# A POSTMODERN TAO

# A POSTMODERN TAO

## A Guide to Apprehending Ways of Meaning in Pathless Lands

Seven Contemplations With Review/Reflection Exercises
For Geography, Philosophy and Science Students

**Jim Norwine**
Texas A&I University

Edited by **Linda Ford Winans**
Tulane University

Foreword by **Steven Bindeman**
Strayer College

UNIVERSITY
PRESS OF
AMERICA

Lanham • New York • London

Copyright © 1993 by
# University Press of America®, Inc.
4720 Boston Way
Lanham, Maryland 20706

3 Henrietta Street
London WC2E 8LU England

**Library of Congress Cataloging-in-Publication Data**

Norwine, Jim.
A postmodern tao : a guide to apprehending ways of meaning in
pathless lands : seven contemplations with review/reflection exercises
for geography, philosophy, and science students / Jim Norwine ;
edited by Linda Ford Winans ; foreword by Steven Bindeman.
p.      cm.
Includes bibliographical references and index.
1. Postmodernism.   2. Tao.   I. Winans, Linda Ford.   II. Title.
B831.2.N69      1993      149—dc20      92–40602 CIP

ISBN 0–8191–8992–8 (cloth : alk. paper)
ISBN 0–8191–8993–6 (pbk. : alk. paper)

 The paper used in this publication meets the minimum requirements of
American National Standard for Information Sciences—Permanence
of Paper for Printed Library Materials, ANSI Z39.48–1984.

FOR

*L*

Giving up the ideal for the real is our only job.

—Andrei Codrescu, *The Disappearance of the Outside*

Forget the vulgar, insultingly patronizing fairy tale that has been hammered into your heads since childhood that the main meaning of life is to be happy. The only true happiness is to share the sufferings of the unhappy.

—Yevgeny Yevtushenko at Juniata College, June 1991

# Contents

# Foreword

Modernism is dead. Its tenets no longer hold. Its conceit, that our experience ultimately makes sense and that the universe is knowable, has become recognized for what it was. Its lenses, through which we saw a clear and distinct image, have been traded in. What we seem to have now is more like a prism, through which we experience only an indirect sense of the incompleteness of our perceptions. The mathematical paradigm of the calculus, which seemingly helped us obtain an approximation of reality, has given way to the matrix, whereby we work with the concept of a system—without always understanding the workings of its parts.

There are arguments about whether postmodernism is a stage in the historical era known as modernism, or whether it is a separate era all its own, with its own code of behavior, its own puzzles, its own paradigms, its own masters. Certainly modernism had gurus—so perhaps postmodernism has anti-gurus. Gurus teach truths; anti-gurus teach how truths fall apart, how we're left with a center that cannot hold itself together, with scattered meanings that never seem to coalesce.

Perhaps more than anything else, postmodernism is an attitude, a flight from certitude. Behind every truth we seem to find a lie (Nietzsche). This attitude seems to pervade much of our current thinking. Physicists once believed that atoms were the ultimate building blocks of nature, which, even though they couldn't be seen, could still be pictured, imagined, and, in some significant ways, understood. But with the twentieth-century discoveries of subatomic particles, physical conditions within the atom, in terms of the forces that hold the nucleus together and keep the electrons from flying away from it, became known. And not only could this world not be seen, neither could it be pictured nor imagined nor even understood in any traditional sense. The system was seen as understandable, but the ultimate relationship between its parts was not. The position and the momentum of a subatomic particle cannot be measured simultaneously. The act of measurement itself interferes with the accuracy of the results. This indeterminacy is a defining feature of the postmodern phenomenon. Certitude, it seems, doesn't even exist in the real world; scientists can't even grasp the parts that make it up.

In the postmodern world, the concept of distance has become blurred. We measure a yard by a yardstick. This is clear (although when the yardstick is made of cloth and it stretches, it's not so clear). But when someone asks us how far is it to go across town, the issue is less clear, since the real issue is not one of distance but of time—since some routes may in fact be shorter "as the crow flies" but they may involve side streets, they may have lots of stoplights, or whatever. Here the shortest distance really means the shortest time. In New York City there is a famous apartment house called the Dakota. (It is in fact the place where John Lennon lived, and it was outside this building that he was shot and killed.) The place is called the Dakota because at the time it was built (in the nineteenth century) it was considered to be so far from downtown New York that it was thought to be "as inaccessible as the Dakotas." (The building is off Central Park West, several miles from downtown.) With a horse and buggy, this was quite a trek, certainly one of several hours. Nowadays, we can get to Paris from New York in about the same amount of time, on the Concorde. Furthermore, in outer space the situation is even more confusing: measurement of distance requires a standard reference point, and there simply isn't one. Reference to a specific space-time continuum still doesn't help us escape from the feelings of arbitrariness and insignificance that come over us when we contemplate our place in the scheme of things.

In the postmodern world, the world has gotten smaller—and more complex as well. The omnipresence of the media has reached such a point that we in the USA often know more about a coup in another country, and more quickly, than the inhabitants in that country themselves. The trouble is that this information which we are constantly acquiring quickly reaches capacity overload in our minds. In an information age, there is simply too much of the stuff around. Moreover, the information we get is often problematic: it's biased, it's disreputable or irrelevant and maybe we don't want to know it or shouldn't ever have had to, or the event was staged just for media consumption, or we know who's going to win the election even before we get a chance to vote, etc. This realization of complexity, that behind every event, behind every fact is a series of complications that fade off into the sunset, is another major feature of the postmodern experience.

Behind every truth is a lie, and behind every genuine feeling there is a moment in a sitcom. Most of us have advertising jingles rattling around in our heads, often at the most inconvenient times. Of all the outgrowths of the media, the phenomenon of television has become the most insidious. Images pass by on the screen, and we confuse them with reality. Sitcom characters become more entertaining than our friends: they have more interesting problems and they're cuter to boot. News programs provide us with a clarity or sense of things that may not exist anywhere else. Remember the "spin doctors" who spoke on network TV after the '88 debates? They "explained" to us what their candidates were "really" saying and doing, all appearances to the contrary. Educators often complain how their students have shorter and shorter attention spans. Since TV has replaced books as our major source of entertainment, our critical skills have ossified, too. Network news programs don't analyze issues much, since sound bites are what sell, not hard analysis; if you want analysis, read a book.

In the postmodern world, people have little patience; they want it now, whatever "it" is. Why do they want it now? Because they are by-products of a media age, and commercials run the media. Commercials tell people what they are supposed to want and when they are supposed to want it. Who would have suspected ten years ago, for example, that there would be an incredible demand for sneakers that cost upwards of $100? Be like Mike. Bo knows. The images combined with these themes are extremely powerful. Few kids can resist them—and few parents can resist their kids' desires forever.

Looking for a final cause, we might turn to the theory of dialectical materialism, which would posit an economic base upon which the superstructure of the commercial world is built. From this point of view, we have become commodity fetishists because we have no choice in the matter; the capitalist system determines that we will be good consumers, and the forces it creates and controls make sure that this status quo is maintained. Exploitation is the name of the game. But for the postmodern sensibility, such thinking is atavistic. There are no final causes; we live in a world of appearances, with no reality behind perceptual experience. (So you think that tennis shoes cost too much? Relative to what? Money has no meaning except in reference to social conditions. When referring to the relative costs of different items, reference must be made to purchasing power. For a person taking home $25,000 a year, the "cost" of the sneakers would be about one-fifth of a week's earnings. But do you want your kid to steal them? Or lose face with friends?) We must also consider that the methodology of dialectical materialism has become suspect due to the recent upheavals in many of the communist societies around the world. Capitalism is in the ascendancy, and the "American Way of Life" reigns supreme—except that this "truth" too falls apart upon further reflection.

Jim Norwine's *A Postmodern Tao* is a collection of interconnected essays and talks in pursuit of "the pattern of our age, a time of the most profound disjunctions of intellectual and spiritual worldviews since the nova of scientific knowledge of about half a millennium ago." Certainly, the author's conception of the path (tao) of geography, for instance, is not what most people would assume: "In geography, the spatial truths one endeavors to recognize are unfolding patterns in the dynamic relations between *Homo sapiens* and Earth." This orientation is enormously influenced by the example of Yi-Fu Tuan, a professor of geography at the University of Wisconsin and the author of numerous books on the interface between geography and the postmodern world. Norwine's thesis is that "a postmodern collision has just occurred between a pair of antithetical 'certainties,' namely, between the modern primacy of the individual and the traditional primacy of the collectivity." These patterns will give rise to "a geographer's quest of ever-receding horizons of understanding." The whole work (and not only Chapter II, which is what he is referring to here) "aspires to be a reconciliation of antinomies, a meeting of themes, and as such, a collage rather than a mere patchwork." Thus Norwine eschews ordinary analysis in favor of the presentation of conflicting themes, a presentation which is intended to reflect the underlying philosophical tensions inherent in the postmodern worldview.

Norwine views himself as a postmodern traveler (never having to leave his armchair due to the ubiquity and reach of contemporary media and computers—although it should be noted that he does include as an appendix several sections that deal with his actual travels around the world) on a pilgrimage in search of those "human geographies" (a term from Yi-Fu Tuan) which draw on the arts with a concern for real human problems, in an effort to create worlds out of this environment. What we get from all of this in the present work is a bewildering "array" (a term I purposely take from matrix algebra since it refers to a presentation of relationships without the assumption of an underlying clarity) of quotations, paraphrases, derivations, lists of texts, epigraphs, and the like, held together by Norwine's commitment to authenticity, to real human problems. This commitment is illustrated by the following: "the destruction of our surroundings stems from our having fallen into an ironically circular syllogistic gyre: although we think we know the earth (i.e., as an assemblage of mineral, gaseous, liquid and recently-deceased biological things available for ready conversion into such useful stuff as sausages, toothpaste dispensers, and lawn flamingoes), we don't understand it at all and, moreover, at an intuitive level we know that we don't understand." Norwine quotes from F. Ferre to suggest that the postmodern scientist "must keep the modern tools of analysis sharp, but in their proper roles as tools," because postmodern science will send the scientist "back into the Garden to work with respect and caution"—the Garden of Eden, I suspect, is a place where things have no names because they have not yet been understood (by modern science) and can thus be examined honestly, without prejudice—this attitude could well be seen as a legacy from the battlefields of modern physics, won, it would seem, by the quantum physicists who broke with the atomic theory that still maintained a continuity with the historically honored assumption that ultimately things make sense, that God does not play dice with the Universe.

That things don't ultimately make sense is a basic assumption of postmodernity. *A Postmodern Tao* does a marvelous job in providing guidelines, or maps, for the further investigation into these conditions. The work's extensive use of quotations and references may seem a bit much, but upon reflection, this technique is entirely appropriate to the spirit of postmodernity, indeed, even an effective methodology in response to the problematic. Norwine demonstrates a kind of faith in the possibilities of future survival and future enlightenment, but only if we are able to turn away from the selfish, manipulative ways in which we commonly address one another, and indeed these are the same ways with which we treat the earth upon which we live.

*A Postmodern Tao* is indeed one of the more successful treatments I have come across on the subject. The author is exceptionally widely read in all areas that pertain to the subject, and if the effect of all this reading and referencing is at first exhausting, the author's practical common sense, and his emphasis on a commitment to standards (in response to the common overemphasis of many critics on postmodernity's tendency towards a proliferation and relativism of values) are ultimately rewarding.

As an appendix the author includes four chapters, entitled "Wanderings," that deal with his travel experiences in Egypt, Iraq, India, and England during the last few years. They serve in some sense as an extension of the readings that precede them; the author almost seems to be testing his philosophy against the real-life experiences that make up the body of these reflections. They are entertaining, humorous, and thought provoking.

Norwine clearly intends his work to be a kind of guide, a map of the various unfoldings of meaning that constitute the postmodern experience. His review/reflection exercises at the end of each chapter display a commitment to showing and doing (as against saying and explaining) that is totally in keeping with the experiential spirit of postmodernism. In a bright and cheerful manner, he shows us the way through a Cyberland in which fact and fiction are all too often one and the same:

> A second ago it would have been easy to grasp a
>     word and repeat it once and then again,
> any one of those phrases one utters alone in a
>     room without mirrors
> to prove to oneself that it's not certain,
>                     that we are still alive after all,
> but now with weightless hands night is lulling the
>     furious tide, and one by one images recede,
>     one by one words cover their faces.
>                         (Octavio Paz, "The Endless Instant")

Seeming to speak of death, Paz's words could also be applied to the postmodern condition, a world in which the light of clarity is receding into the murkiness of complexity, and virtual reality is just beginning to replace actual reality as the vision of choice.  Information—not meaning.

Steven Bindeman
Philosophy
Strayer College

# Preamble:
# Welcome to Cyberland!

Last year continuity and discontinuity were much on my mind. As has been a habit of mine, I transposed the personal problem with its inevitable ambiguities onto the bright-lit stage of an impersonal question. Why make another move? Why cut the roots that one has established, perhaps for the first time in one's life? One answer is that I have always felt that being in place—being rooted—is an illusion. I have always been haunted by the idea of departure both of the glad, self-initiated and of the wrenching, unwilling kind. We are all more or less aware of a final departure that awaits us, but we are less aware of it when we are in the presence of friends and good books and are comforted by their projection of continuity and of reverberating meaning.

— Yi-Fu Tuan, "Continuity and Discontinuity"

In this book, I pursue the patterns of an era, our present age, a time of the most profound disjunctions of intellectual and spiritual worldviews since the nova of scientific knowledge of about half a millennium ago. Specifically, this book is a series of interconnected contemplations or essays in which I reflect on a number of questions I believe to be especially important to those interested in the larger significance of contemporary environmental science, philosophy and geography. To begin with, for example, can an academic "discipline" remain sufficiently coherent to constitute a reason-to-be in Cyberland's[1] centerless mindscapes of the late twentieth century? More worrisome is the question, can *any* centers hold in the absence of centeredness? Can a person even continue to aspire to live the good intellectual and moral life in Cyberland, where it would seem that such a word as *good* could have only a pragmatic and, thus, ironic sense? "Good." Nudge, nudge; wink, wink.

Let me answer a little parabolically. Where I live in Texas the streams and ponds are so thick with mud and silt and assorted goo that they are absolutely opaque. Easily discouraged seekers of fish return home without wetting a hook, for there are no obvious indications of the existence of fish in these waters. However, the persistent and the faithful discover that, as they suspected, there are lots of fine fish here. (This is not to say that they find exactly the fish they expected or desired: catfish or sunfish may turn up in place of bass and trout.) Cyberland too is a murky realm, ever shrouded by the Clouds of Knowing Too Much But Never Enough. It is not possible ever to be completely comfortable or certain in Cyberland, but so what? Consider the difference between the certainty of being in love and the uncertainty experienced deep into a good marriage. The latter, a happy celebration of the otherness of the Other, has a reality which the former lacks and is consequently worth a very great deal of discomfort. Cyberland, I am convinced, is closer to "reality," to whatever truth and meaning are, than any realm we have previously inhabited.

It is, however, as I have conceded, an uncomfortable one. Ours is in particular a very difficult age in which to be a young scholar (or merely to be young, for that matter) because, jaded by the age-old dialectic of philosophy, "essence" versus "existence," and jarred by the recent loss of our favorite certainties, we have begun to lose faith in reality itself and thus in ourselves. This is, at best, a wrong turn leading into a sociophilosophical cul-de-sac. Truth is not only a "pathless land," as Krishnamurti so felicitously put it two generations ago, but a land which always seems to lie just across an ever-receding horizon. Each time our "true knowledge" manages to converge with Truth we have exercised a faith, as naive as it is deep, in the fundamental coherency of reason and experience—and thereby in whatever qualities of Nature empirical data and rationality resonate with or mirror. Our understanding of reality, even quantum reality, "works" because the world, however inconstant and even chaotic, is not capricious. The great mystery is not that the universe is only quasi-describable (e.g., in equations), nor that our knowledge is finite. Rather, the mystery is that there *are* patterns which we *can* begin to understand.

I believe that ultimate significance derives firstly from a respect for and an almost voyeuristic interest in that which is Other, and secondly from the character or quality of one's personal quest for that understanding. I begin with the recognition that the pencil with which I am writing, for example, is different from "me." Respecting its suchness is absolutely essential, for here knowledge begins. As I study it, however, the focus of my attention begins to shift to the fact that the pencil and I are bound to one another and that the pencil may in fact (as I get to know it still better) prove to be more tightly connected to me, perhaps even more *me*, than earlier seemed the case. My first presumption, then, is that in doing my best to understand all of these—the pencil's distinctive pencilness, how we are alike and (especially) the relationship between us—I am aligning myself with meaning and truth.

By way of illustrating the importance of the recognition of otherness, permit me to share a personal experience. On a recent Monday afternoon I was riding my bicycle along a street just south of campus, feeling pretty sorry for myself, for several reasons. First, it was late August, which meant (a) I was broke and it was hot as Hades and (b) I would remain broke and the atmosphere would remain nuclear till October. Second, I had had a day of committee meetings, rendered less tolerable than usual because faculty colleagues had twice managed to behave even more fatuously than the administrators. Third, classes would begin in thirty-six hours and I was forced to face the reality of trying for nine months (a) to be intelligent and (b) not to strangle anyone. Fourth, I was heading home to drink a gallon of the postmodern equivalent of castor oil as preparation for having my lower regions roto-rooted Tuesday in Corpus Christi. (I'll stop at these four, although they are really merely the highlights.)

Please note that, although I have described my mood as self-pity, all of these were in fact quite legitimate reasons to be disgruntled. You may in principle consider the world of *maya* to be illusion, but believe me, when they run several meters of garden hose up your backside, you are likely to perceive the experience as all too real. Anyhow, my point is that I hadn't invented any of these worries.

So, there I am, peddling through the heat, muddling along in spite of two half flat tires, muttering to myself about the injustice of it all, bent low by the weight of my concerns. Suddenly I heard the ferocious barking of a dog as it bounded from behind a car parked to my right and proceeded to charge. My heart thumped and I nearly lost my balance as I turned to see my attacker. Where was he? I couldn't locate the offender until—"Bark, bark, bark!"—I looked down at the street toward the source of the racket. Good Lord! A canine the size of a taco was endeavoring to eat my tire. What *is* this dogito? I wondered. My *nose* is as big as this mutt. As I wobbled on, he gathered himself and jumped mightily into the air, trying to bite my foot, which couldn't have been more than eighteen inches above the ground. "Bark, bark, bark!" he insisted, rushing from one side of me to the other, hoping to find something, anything, small enough to fit in his mouth. "Bark, bark, bark: Stay out of my territory or you're dead meat, huge ugly monster!"

I had to laugh. "O help, help," I cried. "Someone save me!" Several passersby on the nearby sidewalk looked at me strangely; doubtless they couldn't either hear or see the demi-dog. Finally, after a block or so, the poochette was satisfied that I had gotten the message and, with a final threat—"Bark!"—trotted back to the coffee cup or other declivity whence he had come.

I found myself smiling the rest of the day, even though I was still facing the prospect of the academic year, more heat, and my roto-doctor. Why did I smile? Nothing "real" had changed, had it?

There is no point denying that mine is a cosmic view dominated by mystery rather than magic. It is. To believe that the universe depends fundamentally on me, or even on us, seems to me subjective idealism raised (perhaps unavoidably) to the level of solipsism ("I am the only reality"), the postmodernist's saddest face.

I do not aspire to explicate *The* postmodern tao of science or geography or philosophy. That would be a double contradiction in terms. In the first place, more than anything else, *tao* suggests that which is certainly fundamental but even more certainly, mysterious. (Whether tao is more fundamental, or more mysterious, than, say, love is an intriguing question. Quite possibly it isn't, but postmodern hubris has wrought great damage to our ability to appreciate such aspects of reality as love.)

In the second place, although the meanings of "postmodern" and of "The tao" must be conceded to clash at least at the level of the obvious, it is a mistake to conclude that postmodernity and tao are ultimately opposed. Hence *a* postmodern tao. The tortoise beat the hare because it was neither enchanted by Assumptions of The Way Things Must Be nor so filled with despair—"I don't see any meaning to this so it must have no meaning"—that it simply gave up. Journeys into the pathless, placeless realms of significance and truth are sure to be more felicitous after the traveler has abandoned pet certainties.

What I do hope is (1) that this book conveys to the curious the necessity of pursuing a postmodern tao and (2) that, now and again, it exemplifies the spirit of such a tao. I would like to think that as some readers travel these pages they anticipate with a shudder the vistas which lie ahead . . .

As to style, well, Michel de Montaigne not only invented the essay, he set a standard for transparent, informative and entertaining prose which many have striven to emulate. I suppose I fancy myself to be among those aspirants, although the essays which are the chapters in this book are more like meditative polemics and, so, more art than science. Personal reverie, as well as the focus and quality of the sharing of that reverie, is in this context more important than depth of analysis.

Finally, in spite of the serious reservations about postmodernism I express in these chapters, I must in good conscience mutter—just audibly, hoping that you've already skipped ahead to the Introduction—this admission: My title is a confession. *A Postmodern Tao* is a postmodernist's book. It is too consistently baroque, playfully Pickwickian and—especially—thoroughly subversive of existing "postmodern" assumptions to be anything else.

## Note

1.   My somewhat subversive use of *Cyberland* to refer to postmodernity's decentered, placeless spaces which we increasingly occupy—participating in a computer network is an obvious example—is of course based only very loosely on Norbert Weiner's "cybernetics" and William Gibson's "cyberspace." I particularly wish to convey the importance of contingency, relation and system in the new episteme, and the consequent importance to the individual of understanding and then consciously charting a personal course through such a mindscape. To use a simple illustration, it is possible for an individual caught in a quasi-cybernetic system to pursue in terms of "ultimate ends" a significant life as an employee of the United States Postal Service, but to do so it is necessary to utilize an awareness which the system lacks.

Others may prefer *hyperspace* rather than *Cyberland*, but the former I think conjures an image of above or beyond rather than *different*.

# Acknowledgments

Truism though it may be, the shortcomings of this work *do* owe entirely to my scholarly mistakes and personal limitations, while credit for its merits largely *do* belong to other people. In particular, I owe much to the examples of two masters of faith-keeping, Yi-Fu Tuan and Peter Gould. To Linda Ford Winans, another resolutely ingenuous soul, for her penetrating and cruelly loving editing, and for her contributions to the Review and Reflection questions that follow each chapter: thank you. Thanks also to Hazel Lautz Ibáñez for her word-processing wizardry. And, answering the question—how many Aggies does it take to enlighten a provincial pest?—at least two: many thanks to Jerry North of the Texas A&M University Climate System Research Program for his support, moral and material, and to A&M's Manuel Davenport, for an inspired course in contemporary philosophy.

I gratefully acknowledge the reading of early drafts by the following: Steven Bindeman, Strayer College, Washington, D.C.; Daniel Botkin, Department of Biology and Environmental Studies, University of California, Santa Barbara; Kenneth Boulding, Professor Emeritus, Department of Economics, University of Colorado, the Reverend Michael Ensrude; David Greegor, Idaho Department of Water Resources, Boise; David Ray Griffin, Claremont, California; Peter Gould of the Department of Geography at Pennsylvania State University; Terry Jordan, Department of Geography, The University of Texas at Austin; Ian King, Department of Political Science, Hendrix College, Conway, Arkansas; Lester Milbrath, Research Program in Environment and Society, State University of New York at Buffalo; John Rappole, Conservation and Research Center, Smithsonian Institute, Front Royal, Virginia; the late Reverend Sherwood Reisner, Kingsville, Texas; Michael Preda, Political Science, Midwestern State University, Wichita Falls, Texas; Bill Stonebarger; G. Tyler Miller, Jr.; Yevgeny Yevtushenko; Rupert Sheldrake; Andrei Codrescu; Jonathan Mark Smith, Department of

Geography, Texas A&M University, College Station; Brian Swimme, Holy Names College, Oakland, California; Yi-Fu Tuan, Department of Geography, The University of Wisconsin at Madison; David Turner, Department of Anthropology, University of Toronto; my colleagues at Texas A&I University Armando Arias, Robert Davidson, Ron Hamm, Sandy Hicks, Manuel Ibáñez, Michael Jordan, Fernando Rodriguez, Maurice Schmidt, David Deacon, David Laughlin and Bruce Schueneman; and my wife, for her example and for all those Texian qualities I have tried to convey in Chapter VII.

An excerpt from "Iraq" (Appendix: Wanderings) was published under the title "Political Geography" in the December 21, 1990, issue of *The Texas Observer* and appears here in a more complete form by permission of that journal. "The Tao of Geography" appeared in the Winter 1992/93 issue of *The Explorers Journal* (official quarterly of The Explorers Club), and is reprinted here in somewhat revised form with permission. The excerpts from *I and Thou* by Martin Buber, translated by Ronald Gregor Smith, © 1958 Charles Scribner's Sons, and from *Beyond Tragedy* by Reinhold Niebuhr, copyright 1937 Charles Scribner's Sons (copyright renewed [©] 1965 Reinhold Niebuhr), appear by permission of Macmillan Publishing Company. Permission to quote from *The Disappearance of the Outside* by Andrei Codrescu (© 1990) was granted by Addison-Wesley Publishing Company, Reading, Massachusetts. An excerpt from *The Innocent Anthropologist* by Nigel Barley (© 1989) appears by permission of The University of Chicago Press. *Desert Solitaire* by Edward Abbey (© 1968) is quoted by permission of Don Congdon Associates, Inc. (estate of Edward Abbey). *Under the Net* by Iris Murdoch (© Viking 1964) is quoted by permission of Penguin USA. *Seventy Letters* by Simone Weil (trans. Sir Richard Rees, Oxford, © 1965) is quoted by permission of Oxford University Press. *The Immense Journey* by Loren Eiseley (© Random House 1957), *Creation* by Gore Vidal (© Ballantine 1986) and *Possession* by A.S. Byatt (© Random House 1990) are all quoted by permission of Random House, Inc. In addition, various short poetic, expository and narrative quotations have been excerpted to complement and enrich the flow and thrust of my words. I very gratefully acknowledge the authors and publishers of those brief passages. It is my hope that I "repay" them by introducing some readers to their fine work. Humble thanks are also extended to those whose ideas I've referred to or borrowed. I have striven to fully acknowledge each of you, but where I've overlooked or inadvertently misrepresented someone's thinking, I apologize. I ask my readers to write to me about any such deficiencies so that future editions may be corrected.

# Introduction

In this world space no longer exists, for in every place, everything is possible; man is everywhere at once, for he may always stay and, at the same time, still be in flight. The identical possibilities are diffused throughout space, which is thus abolished.

—Max Picard, *The Flight from God*

"You are a maker of bronze. You want to cast a bell, and you have prepared a crucible for the molten metal. But when you pour out the fiery metal, the bronze refuses to flow. It says, 'No, I don't want to be a bell. I want to be a sword, like the flawless sword of Wu.' As a bronzemaker, you would be most distressed with this naughty metal, wouldn't you?"

"Yes. But metal may not choose its mold. The smelter has that choice."

"No." The softly spoken no was as chilling in its effect as Gosala's thrown string. "You may not rebel against the Way any more than your hand can rebel against your arm or the metal against the mold. All things are a part of the universe, which is the always-so."

—Gore Vidal, *Creation*

It is salutary to remind ourselves that [the mutual relationship between Nature and human cultures], which has long been loftily proclaimed as the essence of Geography, is still relegated too much to the realm of lip-service, over-shadowed by self-contained "human" and "physical" geographies only marginally and formally connected with each other philosophically and practically, even as the world, and matters of life and death, make them increasingly inseparable.

—David Hooson, "Clarence Glacken: In Memoriam"

Alfred North Whitehead believed that the greatest intelligence is required to see the obvious. The obvious is elusive, for as Krishnamurti said, Truth is forever a "pathless land." Thus, discovering a tao or way of understanding seems paradoxically to necessitate a process wherein one *creates* one's own path to knowledge.

For instance, in geography—my scholarly field—the spatial truths one endeavors to recognize are unfolding patterns in the dynamic relationships between *Homo sapiens* and Earth. These typically are so complex (i.e., profoundly influenced by place and time), subtle, multi-dimensional, and intrinsically fuzzy that geographers try to be especially attuned to undercurrents and counter-currents, to (for example) the too-obvious-to-register, to common sense and to the counter-intuitive, as possible hints or clues or harbingers. As *tao* itself implies that which lies behind the apparent order of things, so too the tao of geography refers especially to those patterns which support, and deny, the obvious.

Some postmodern scholars seem to conclude, as the Buddha did twenty-five hundred years ago, that in the stream that is Nature there exists no constant, no certainty, no Truth even, save flux itself. The very idea of centers is seen as a mythic fabrication. Consequently, according to critics like Hardison (1989), history and—by implication—geography, philosophy and all the other academic "disciplines" have disappeared like phantoms through postmodernity's "skylight."

Change is Nature's preeminent observable hallmark: whirl is king, as Aristophanes said. To speak the truism that no one can step into the same river twice, however, is not to suggest that there is no river. Like the waves, vortices and currents in any stream, the unrelenting fluxes which we witness and experience are evanescent concentrations, assemblages and configurations of an irreducible river of existence which we can characterize as tao.

Tao admittedly is a metaphor nearly as inadequate as, say, energy. To argue whether we should call the universe's irreducible "breath" (simply an older image than energy, no real difference) form or thing, essence or existence, is—if I may steal a line from Calvin of comic-strip fame—to fail to appreciate the unimaginable wonder that it *is*.

Every tao is grounded in that virtue which accrues to an innocent sense of wonder, a humility skeptical of claims to certainty and—paradoxically—a faith in at least the possibility of access to the Always-So. Recall Thomas Mann's "plastic irony":

> The unflinching eye detects, the intellect names, the heart goes out
> in compassion; and the life-force of every life-loving heart will be
> finally tested, challenged and measured by its capacity to regard with
> compassion whatever has been by the eye perceived and by the
> intellect named. (Quoted in Campbell 1972)

A generation ago, most humanists and social scientists were certain that the world was shrinking, that multiple worldviews were converging, collapsing into a single commonality of blue jeans and Big Macs. This idea proved inadequate, for it overestimated the leveling power of technology and democracy. Today, the accent is on cultural *difference*. Cultural diversity has become the anthem of humanism. A refreshing change, yes; but *any* paradigm is impoverished by an assumption of certainty, especially that of a personal autonomy isolated from the touchstone of community. Pluralism and diversity carried to the extreme evoke an absurdly egalitarian world of six billion equally valid self-contained movements disconnected from the need to serve any larger symphony. Although difference offers both metaphysical and practical potencies which sameness lacks, it is nevertheless not always superior to sameness nor is it even always desirable.[1]

A postmodern collision has just occurred between a pair of antithetical "certainties," namely, between the modern primacy of the individual and the traditional primacy of the collectivity. In the first decades of the third millennium, the shape of our world will be determined by one or both of two possible vectors created by that collision.

The first of these vectors is downward and backward. It combines the conformity of tribalism (machismo, for instance) with a narcissistic solipsism ("I am the only reality"). Haiti, the Punjab, the former Soviet "Union," Sri Lanka, Peru, Liberia and Yugoslavia could be but harbingers of a very dark age if this nightmarish synthesis comes to dominate the next century.

The second vector represents a harmonious complementarity of self and other. Its course, upward and forward, is toward meaning, which always lies, to paraphrase Jacob Needleman (1970), at the conjunction of the "real world" of things, and self, with that of Other.

In seeking to find and to follow those emerging patterns of meaning which comprise, or at least point toward, postmodern taos, we pursue what Saint Augustine called the "source of the light of reason." By its very nature, that beacon cannot be located exclusively in the phenomenal realm of the individual self. Nor can it be found strictly within the collectivity, not even in that ultimate noumenal tribe, the One. Our potentialities and significances—maybe even our "purposes"—occur exclusively, as Needleman has suggested, on the Way which bridges the perceived chasm between the worlds of existence and essence.

In this little volume I share a philosophical geographer's quest of ever-receding horizons of understanding. A friend once laughingly dismissed my *Weltanschauung* as one of "romantic science." My reply is that my friend, like so many of our contemporaries, has acceded to one of the more egregious errors in twentieth-century philosophy of science in accepting the necessity and totality of the "break" proposed by Gaston Bachelard ([1934] 1968) between logos or *science*—the domain of objectivity, intellect and reason—and mythos or *reverie*—the realm of mystery, imagination and art (Bhaskar 1989; Short 1992).[2]

Although I rejoice in the delights of modern technodemocracy in a way the romantic poets mostly did not, I do confess considerable sympathy with the spirit as well as the beauty of the *cris de coeur* of Rousseau, Wordsworth and Eliot. Still, as Kenneth Boulding once said, an angel with a flaming sword stands guard at the entrance to innocence (1980). There is no way back to ignorance. The longing to "return" to Nature is as futile a wish as hoping for wings. (More futile, really: it's only a matter of time till people *do* have wings, if only via virtual computer systems.)

The challenge of the third millennium shall be far more profound than any simple-minded positivist, romantic *or* deconstructionist ever dreamed, for it shall require some manner of reconciliation of modernity's complexity, dynamism, autonomy and limitless "democracy of possibilities" with the regularities, patterns and essential simplicity which mirror the Always-So. Whatever the shortcomings of this volume, I will count it a success if it encourages some readers to attempt that reconciliation.

All of these essays (except the appended "Wanderings") were born as public lectures delivered between 1989 and 1991. Because the majority of my readers will, I think, be university undergraduates, in each chapter (but in several much more than in others) I have attempted to retain a measure of the playfulness, informality and directness of the familiar, conversational voice of the visiting lecturer. And in the spirit of the professor who prefers to provoke reflection rather than prescribe formulaic responses, much of what I say here is, in the words of one reader, "coherent but intentionally unclear—prosaic poetry." (Recalling Neville Dane's remark somewhere that poetry mustn't be "about" anything, perhaps "prosaic poetry" isn't far off the mark.) The rambling, allusive style is part of my design to stimulate contemplation of the complex and the simple simultaneously; some passages are not meant to go down easily but rather, I hope, will invite the reader to pause and chew on the words a bit, explore the mixtures of substance and spice, turn them on the tongue with open curiosity, and perhaps acquire a taste for exotic, undefinable flavors of thought. If the style seems at times almost baroque, I beg the reader's indulgence. Like distant stars, the truly important is probably best approached obliquely. (Here lies the power of parables over prescriptions.) More importantly, the disarming subversion of what appears, at the level of the obvious, to be merely flippant irreverence is the postmodernist's most effective device for suggesting not only that the personal pursuit of truth and meaning remains what the well-lived life is all about, but that the fuzzier and more remote truth and meaning seem, the closer they actually are. (Should you be dubious of this ploy, I suggest that you study carefully a few episodes of "The Simpsons.")

Among the persuasions gathered here as discrete "chapters," two of the brood are quite different from the other hatchlings and are also distinctly unlike each other. Firstly, the appended "Wanderings" are excerpts from a traveler's journal, which occasionally reveal, I hope, a dollop of Mann's plastic irony. That is their intent, to exemplify a manner of compassionate observing, thinking and writing.

Secondly, Chapter II ("A Map is Not the Territory"), which is the least original of these offerings, may be the most deserving of attention. It is a collection of thoughts and—more importantly—metaphors and images shared with the willing reader. It aspires to be a reconciliation of antinomies, a meeting of themes, and as such a collage rather than a mere patchwork. Notwithstanding the success or failure of this quilt, however, nearly all its patches are memorable, many are beautiful, and more than a few are wrenching metaphors which offer no less than the "shock of the real" (Abbey 1968).

*A Postmodern Tao* is on balance no better than a limited success, I think, for the simple reason that even the likes of G. K. Chesterton or William James would have been hard pressed to fathom and "explain" the turn of this millennium. The tough question isn't, Will post-mystery, post-meaning people become jerks?—the answer to that one seems self-evident; i.e., to a shocking degree, we already are jerks. The truly engaging question is, What's next? Where do we go from here? Who are we to be, if not merely ever-cleverer jerkmeisters-of-the-universe?

It could be that the next great step-function in "human" evolution will be in some measure post-human (where human=*Homo sapiens*): technology and democracy may well have brought us to the end of a strictly human history. Although I am worried that we will be almost literally enchanted, or anesthetized, by the brilliant fakery of such technologies as virtual reality (see Chapter II), perhaps we'll need a little help from our machine friends to shortcircuit the pleasure-alienation feedback loop in which we seem to be mired.

Still, if this book is but a limited success, it does I think speak in its playful vernacular to a number of unfolding patterns the understanding of which is essential to comprehending contemporary states of mind and being. For example, the decentering which virtually defines our times is far deeper and more profound than any mere "browning" of North America and Europe, a misreading of which not a few much more substantial works are guilty. However painful the process in the short term, I believe it self-evident that "mongrelizing" each other is sure to be beneficial, if not universally, then at least in most ways to most people. If in A.D. 2100 we are neither jerks nor cyborgs, I suspect that it will be because of this process.

No, we are in the early stages of a vastly more radical transformation, one better compared to the scientific nova of half a millennium ago or even to the beginning of agriculture (and, thus, of cities) nearly 10,000 years ago, to the Sumerian invention of writing about 2,000 B.C. or to the Europeanization of the New World (really, one might as well say "of the world") of recent centuries. This is I think no less than the death of one age and the birth of another. *A Postmodern Tao* will succeed to the extent that it helps its readers to grasp and accept this reality and to prepare to deal with its implications. Postmodern ways to truth are manifold, potentially as limitless and varied as knowledge itself, for our conscious actions of discovering and following these paths help create, or at least unfold, them.

It is consequently not surprising that most "timeless truths" have lost their efficacy. (Consider that even our "spin" on some of the Ten Commandments is already essentially ironic: e.g., honoring the Sabbath or even one's father and mother.) What I find more interesting are those few—not revelations but, let us say—*intuitions* about truth which have undeniable potency.[3] Firstly (for instance) the greater our knowledge the more we still find the horizon between ourselves and that which we seek receding. Consider the nearly ubiquitous tension experienced today between the common-sense certainties of life, on the one hand, which obtain even for contemporary philosophers and literary theorists (e.g., I am writing this sentence *now* although I can't define *now* and in fact it's already gone; or, a Toyota is better than a Yugo; or, a cold beer and hot pretzel at a fiercely contested ball game are preferable to hemorrhoids; or, a helping hand is superior to murder; and so forth), and, on the other hand, the realization, even by those who don't know a signified from a signifier and who could care less, that the connections between Being and our words and images have become so frayed that even the most centered of us begin in our heart of hearts to doubt the real. Viewed thusly postmodern taos are far more unearthly and less explicable than Lao-tsu's charmingly simple *Tao Te Ching*.

Secondly, it is evident that our multiple taos will be not only every bit as elusive but as exclusive as ever the Tao was. The equality of kitsch is the latest in a long line of alluring denials. "Anything goes" or "I can have it all": this is faith in ignorance over knowledge, first cousin to Santa Claus, the Easter Bunny and prayers that two plus two equal anything but four.

Of the Tao's ancient resonances, the final and most painful—"For God's sake, shut up!" we cry punfully, covering our ears—is that the gate *is* narrow. Magical thinking is appropriate to the demon-filled dark places of the simple and the young, but for those of us who long since should have come of age it is unbecoming in every sense of the word.

## Notes

1. The Africanized ("killer") bees, which have just invaded the region in which I reside, South Texas, provide a useful reminder of the reality of what might be thought of as *negative heterogeneity*. Thirty years after their escape in Brazil, and contrary to various forms of scholarly and popular wishful thinking, the bees—which remain as aggressive as ever—will in coming decades almost certainly wreak havoc with sunbelt agriculture generally and the commercial honey industry specifically, restrict outdoor activity (especially on the part of the very young and the very old), and seriously injure many people.

2.   Anyhow, better a romantic science than the implied solipsism of contemporary "idealistic" science, according to which no reality could exist except via us. I wish I could recall who wrote, quite recently, that only people who spend all day indoors could so blithely defy common sense.

3.   This is true of the injunction against killing, I think, notwithstanding the frequent meanness of our present behavior.

# I.  The Tao of Geography

*Chi fuor li maggior tui?*:  What is the nature of your journey across time?
Out of what world did you arrive?
— George Steiner, *Real Presences*

$A$ll the American geographers I know still love the idea of travel (thank God).  Somehow, though, many of us have fallen out of the habit of actually *going* places.  Worse yet, when we do happen to venture outside, we often seem to forget that real traveling is much more like a walk in the park than, say, a nonstop flight from Kansas City to Khartoum.  A journey, like any other process of discovery, must provide opportunities for rambling, or else it becomes something like a walk down the hall to the W.C.:  useful, but not necessarily instructive.[1]

I was reminded of this the other evening while watching an episode of "Star Trek."  The *Enterprise* has happened onto a very wise and gentle stranger who, as it turns out, is a representative of a highly advanced species.  The alien explains that he is a "traveler."

"Where are you going?" he is asked.

"Oh, no PLACE.  Merely through time and space," he replies.

"But why?" the captain demands.

The stranger shrugs.  "Curiosity?" he ventures.

This ingenuous starman appeals, I think, because his is the innocence which has always been the distinctive hallmark of scholar-travelers since, and no doubt long before, the three magi.  Daring to be naive, they remind us of a truism of geography at once so fundamental and so obvious that most geographers seem to overlook it:  journeys—like life—are *ends*, rather than the *means* we too often take them to be.

It is sad to contemplate how anachronistic this notion sounds in the West of these closing years of the second millennium, when virtually every

1

social system and function—from politics to jogging to religion, exclusive (arguably) of sex—has become little more than a means to an end. It is as though, having rejected such "truths" as flat earth, phlogiston, and Aryan superiority, we have lost faith in the very idea of coherency. This is pragmatism mutating beyond even cynicism to, one fears, decadence.

The flaw in this metaphysic is that most human beings intuit the existence of what Robert Pirsig (1974) calls *quality*: that (for example) love is somehow absolutely and intrinsically beautiful. We still sense that a genuine smile is a better gift than a frown. Consider that even in mathematics (that *sine qua non* of empiricism), theories which "smile"—i.e., beautiful theories—are preferred to inelegant explanations. A journey, like a smile, is a naive exercise in faith whose benefits lie in the process itself. Joy and enlightenment equally are the journey's—and the smile's—true raison d'être.

A curious contradiction resounds here: since a generation or so ago most professional geographers and many other social scientists (myself included) became spatial theoreticians-cum-statisticians and—some of us—deconstructionists for whom "metanarratives are 'out'" (Short 1992); of late we have begun to resemble no one so much as the nineteenth-century armchair types we hold in such low esteem. All the new "prosthetic devices of the mind"—personal computers, word processors, satellite imagery, coefficients of correlation and so forth—are vastly more efficient as information-gatherers than are such archaic tools as books, maps, personal journals and writing desks. Even if it is true that the new toys can at times feel eerily like artifacts of a post-human age, they are here to stay. Like Galileo's telescope, they expand our individual and collective horizons. And who among us would trade a hologram of, say, a hurricane for a line drawing of one? About as many, I think, as would give up fire.

A hologram of a hurricane is not, however, a hurricane. High-tech, "faux" observations of complex natural phenomena are such marvelous proxies that, as Kenneth Boulding once remarked about numbers, we sometimes forget that they are not real (1980). It is true that our cerebral skills with respect to the topology of the universe are, alas, sadly limited. For example, in my mind's eye I can see only a very few bowling pins—five, perhaps—simultaneously at any single moment, and these imperfectly. This does not, however, mean we shouldn't from time to time do our best to imagine the actual shapes and sizes of things.

The new virtual computer technology (such as that portrayed in Stephen King's 1992 film *Lawnmower Man*) promises to transcend this shortcoming with such stunning power that we might very well prefer—given our track record with television and video games—a mediated virtual reality to the real. Why go to Paris, one may ask, if one's computer offers the sensation of actually being in the Louvre? In twenty or twenty-five years, when virtual reality or cyberspace is a commonplace, why not follow Dr.

Timothy Leary's latest prescription and "plug in" rather than actually travel? "You won't even need to pack a toothbrush."

A toothbrush seems little more than a means to a specific end: clean teeth. (There's more to it than that, of course. Having to brush our teeth day after day is a sort of prison wherein we are reminded that, thank God, we are not yet gods.) The true worth of travel and of all the important human experiences, however, lies in the process. Life itself is the best example. Consider on a more modest scale the difference between a romantic encounter with another person and masturbation. Masturbation, the experts inform us, transports one to higher immediate levels of gratification because one is in total control of the process. Entertainment unpolluted by extraneous influences, i.e., others.

Besides being aesthetically unsavory, this sensibility is triply flawed. Firstly, entertainment is fine but it is after all *entertainment*. We are so thoroughly a part of a shop-till-you-drop world that it becomes easy—almost necessary, perhaps—to take the trivial for the significant. Secondly, if material reality is somehow, as the Hindus teach, maya or illusion, it also has or manifests a presence worthy of respect. Circling sharks are little impressed by denial of their reality. Thirdly, because my connection to another person—e.g., a kiss—or *any* Other is partly out of my control, it has the potential to be surprising, to jar me into empathy with that which is not me.

"Remotely" apprehending the world from our labs and offices and satellites offers limited but, up to a point, quite reasonable and useful images. After all, if one wants to know, for instance, how many people there are in Calcutta, one relies on published census data, not on impressions formed wandering the city's streets. However, what if one aspires to an understanding of the nature of day-to-day life in Calcutta? Or an understanding of Calcutta's "soul". . . ? There is a limit to how much one can learn from mere facts, as any geographer who has had to teach a course on a region he or she has never visited will verify.

This limitation exists for several reasons. For one, the world is far too messy and chaotic a place ever to be exactly measured. Boulding's famous dictum that "all important distinctions are unclear" (1980) expresses this frustration. Just when you think that you have nailed down the horizon between male and female, plant and animal, living and nonliving, or matter and energy, the rules seem to change. As some sage said, knowledge is always finite, ignorance terribly infinite.

As quick-and-dirty, simple models go, we could do (and have done) worse than apprehending the world as though it were the exposed hardware of some vast computer driven by linear software. This approximation of the universe as logical, measurable and predictable has been a cornerstone of Western scientific and technical progress. But we shouldn't be surprised when the system's programming turns out to be obscure. When, for instance, we encounter beauty and grace and other "strange stuff" in the world (a felicitous phrase which I think belongs to writer Annie Dillard), they turn out to be impossible to reduce to easy units, yet essential to understanding the operation of the system.

Like it or not, we find that to truly know something—a nation or a city or even an anthill—requires some form of participation, if only of an indirect, intellectual variety. As John Wheeler has written of quantum mechanics, in some quixotic sense the universe is "participatory" (1973). For the traveler, imagination, curiosity and wonder are as much requisites as are observation and experience. And because of the sheer volume of information inundating us at present, a sense of wonder may be more important now than ever before.

And so we venture out into the states of mind and of being which are the world, to pry, to speculate, and to participate. If successful, we find that we have left not only home and hearth but, in a sense, ourselves. We expect our journeys to teach us about "them," and so they do. Curiously, however, by looking outward for a little while we find that we learn even more about our own personal myths and worldviews. This is because coming to grips with our own existence is a bit like trying to see a dim star. Peek obliquely and it appears; gaze directly at it and it disappears. Real travel, as defined by Richard Holmes, is concerned with "disorientation" rather than with mere distance, with "losing yourself, and then finding yourself again: casting yourself, at least for one moment, into the lap of the gods, if only to see what happened" (1984).

## Afterwords

Because each journey is unique, anything that the traveler would presume to say about it must inevitably be both personal and qualitative, a one-person's-eye-view of Indianapolis, Ionia, or India. So what? Eleanor Munro wrote recently, quoting Teilhard de Chardin, that one is not always aware just how close a relationship exists between research and a subjective emotional need (1987).

The exchange of distinctive world- and self-views is priceless even though—or, perhaps, because—what is of value and wisdom to one person seems nonsense to another, as Siddhartha put it (Hesse [1922] 1951). It is precisely in the disclosure—confession, almost—of the traveler's subjective and distinctly personal experience that the value of his or her chronicle lies. Richard Holmes (1984) quotes a memorable passage from Robert Louis Stevenson's journal notes of 25 September 1878, when Stevenson and his donkey were rambling across the Massif Central of southern France:

Why anyone should desire to go to Cheylard or to Luc is more than my much inventing spirit can embrace. For my part, I travel not to go anywhere, but to go; I travel for travel's sake. And to write about it afterwards—if only the public will be so condescending as to read. But the great affair is to move; to feel the needs and hitches of life a little more nearly; to get down off this feather bed of civilization, and to find the globe granite underfoot and strewn with cutting flints.

One thinks of such an account as the geographical equivalent of mathematical philosopher Rudy Rucker's essay-allegories (1983), which transform quantum mechanics into something Walt Disney would have known and loved. Although few in number, such literary adventures do exist: outstanding recent examples would include, for instance, Tony Horwitz's *Baghdad Without A Map* (1991); David Chaffetz's *A Journey in Afghanistan* (1981); Bruce Chatwin's *In Patagonia* (1977); *Maps and Dreams*, by Hugh Brody (1982); *Granta*'s special "Travel Writing" issues (e.g., 1984, 1987); Guy Davenport's *The Geography of the Imagination* (1981); Jan Morris's *Destinations* (1980); Francis Steegmuller's *Flaubert in Egypt* (1972); and, Natalie Goldberg's marvelous little vade mecum for the would-be writer, *Writing Down the Bones* (1986).[2]

These literary adventurers share with us their private revelations—here of harmony, there of dissonance; now of entropy, then of unfolding pattern—which, however modest, offer us a temporary asylum from our own clamorous and dizzying vortex. At their best, they offer a larger, more collective perspective of the sublime and the ridiculous, a sort of Brahma's-eye-view rather than our usual limited individual viewpoint.

The literary explorer writes, then, not exactly to teach but, in the words of Hazrat Inayat Khan, "to show them all I see" (1978). The real worth of the showing lies not in its "rightness" but in its innocent, uncompromising honesty. As to accuracy and wisdom, readers will make their own judgments.

Even when the traveler's private vision is flawed, as it inevitably must be, it can be instructive. As Picasso observed, the whole point of an artistic "lie" is to teach the truth. A Monet is deceptive but never insincere or fake. It tricks us in order to reveal to us not merely landscapes of being but those of mind and soul as well. Ultimately, paraphrasing Richard Holmes and Robert Louis Stevenson, every literary adventure is a kind of autobiographical pilgrimage.

The literary pilgrim shares access into her own mindscapes, the best of which, while perhaps still humbler than a Monet, may be a bit less *entre nous*. At the very least, they represent first-hand experience, which is always, as Alfred North Whitehead put it, the key to the intellectual life (quoted by Bakko 1989).

This, then, is my *cri de coeur* to those who would seek to understand and convey the true patterns of geography. It is a plea in favor of Thomas Mann's principle of "plastic irony"—i.e., for perception infused with compassion (Campbell 1972)—for literary adventuring—experential, contemplative, and profoundly personal evocations of the world's states of mind and being—and, finally, for "human geographies" which draw on literature and the arts, but always in association with real, and indeed urgent, human problems and concerns—with the ceaseless human effort to create "worlds" out of "environment" and the anguish and puzzle that inevitably arise from that effort (Tuan 1990b).

## Notes

1.   A "journey" must in some significant measure be *surprising*, i.e., must temporarily jolt one out the solipsistic space virtually all of us inhabit much of the time. A significant part of the experience of discovery is the realization of one's own contingency and redundancy. (These may in turn also prove to be illusions, but at least they are higher ones.)  So-called travel otherwise is at best touristic diversion (e.g., weekend bus excursions to the Catskills or Las Vegas; pretty harmless stuff, really), and at worst, exercises in narcissistic mirror-polishing. The latter—self-reification in the garb of seeking after Other—are worse than nothing. Better to watch an episode of Donahue or Geraldo.

2.   A personal "recipe" would additionally include the following: *All the Pretty Horses* by Cormac McCarthy; *Kabloona* and *A Chinese City* by Gontran de Poncins; Peter Mayle's *A Year in Provence* and *Toujours Provence*; Eleanor Munro's *On Glory Roads*;  Guy Davenport's *Every Force Evolves a Form*;  *Whereabouts: Notes on Being a Foreigner* by Alastair Reid; *Flatland* by Edwin A. Abbott;  Heinrich Harrer's *Seven Years in Tibet*;  *Last Letters from Hav* by Jan Morris;  *A Short Walk in the Hindu Kush* by Eric Newby; Patrick Leigh Fermor's *A Time of Gifts*  and *Between the Woods and Water*;  *The Solace of Open Spaces* by Gretel Ehrlich;  Frances Trollope's *Domestic Manners of the Americans*;  *Far Away and Long Ago* by W. H. Hudson;  *Brazilian Adventure* by Peter Fleming;  Mary Taylor Simeti's *On Persephone's Island*;  *The Songlines* by Bruce Chatwin; *The Light Garden of the Angel King* by Peter Levi; *The Tenants of Time* by Thomas Flanagan;  Edward Rutherfurd's *Sarum*;  Isak Dinesen's *Out of Africa*; *Their Heads are Green* by Paul Bowles; Rachel Carson's *The Sense of Wonder*; *The Oregon Trail* by Francis Parkman, Jr.;  Verlyn Klinkenborg's *The Last Fine Time*; and, Stephen Crane's journalistic sketches, such as "The Broken Down Van," which appeared in *The New York Tribune* in 1892. Stir, simmer, then season with Carl Zuckmayer's *A Part of Myself* and George Eliot's *Middlemarch*. . .

## Review and Reflections on the Text

1.   Define solipsistic; pragmatism; empiricism; *cri de coeur*.

2.   The author lists several human enterprises which are frequently seen as means rather than the ends which they properly should be:  journeying, politics, jogging, education, religion.  Can you think of other examples of this tendency toward confusion of ends and means, or of higher- and lower-order values?  Reflect in writing on your understanding of one or more of the above—or of your own alternative examples—as ends in themselves.

3.   Would you trade a hologram of Paris for a trip to Paris?  How about Ethiopia?  How about a hurricane?  Explore in writing the reasons for your choices.

4.   Have you ever traveled to a place which you had previously studied or heard about and, after arriving, found the real place different from what you expected?  Reflect in writing about how your expectations developed, how the actual experience unfolded, and how your experience was different from your expectations.  Think also about the extent to which your expectations may have affected your responses to the place itself, how they may have influenced what you did and did not notice, and how your responses may have influenced the specific things you chose to do and see in the place or affected the people with whom you interacted there.

5.   Think about the model of the world-as-computer.  In what ways does the analogy "work"?  In what ways doesn't it?  Can you think of other analogies that people have used to describe the world?  What are the strengths and weaknesses of these other analogies?  Which one(s) do you prefer, and why?

6.   The author suggests that "to truly know something. . . requires some form of participation."  Think of instances or activities in your own experience that bear out this assertion.  Can you think of anything that can be "truly known" without participation?

7.   Discuss one or two of your favorite literary adventures.  (If you don't have one or can't think of one, read some excerpts from the works suggested by the author.)  Devote some time to writing down your reflections about the insights or questions that these works have stimulated in you.

8.   In what sense can a flawed vision be instructive?

9.    Explain how an impressionistic painting can be deceptive but not deceitful, a truth-teaching lie?

10.    The author uses the curious term "self-reification" in a note on the greater authenticity of some travels over others which he seems to consider somehow false. Is "self-reification" not a contradiction in terms? To reify is to transform the abstract into the concrete or tangible. Does the author think we don't believe in ourselves? Consider this: If this is a solipsistic age, as the author suggests repeatedly in this book, what is the next logical belief-step after "I am the only reality"?

# II.  A Map is Not the Territory: The Virtue of Reality[*]

The pure taste of the apple is as much a contact with the beauty of the Universe as the contemplation of a picture by Cezanne.

—Simone Weil, *Seventy Letters*

A twenty-five-year-old Japanese girl who achieved enlightenment after some five years of *zazen*: "In the whole universe I am supreme, and it is perfectly natural. I am astonished that I am that One. How wonderful, how marvelous!" Her Zen master's comments: "An ancient Zen saying has it that to become attached to one's own enlightenment is as much a sickness as to exhibit a maddeningly active ego. Indeed, the profounder the enlightenment, the worse the illness. My own sickness lasted almost ten years."

—R. C. Zaehner, *Zen, Drugs and Mysticism*, quoting P. Kapleau, *The Three Pillars of Zen*

*Scene: circa 2008, an American middle-class family's first week with its new personal virtual-reality (pvr) machine. Mr. and Mrs. America have only to don electronic helmets and gloves (or perhaps they have the deluxe electronic bodysuit) to be transported instantly via computer circuitry to—no, into—any one of dozens of alternative experiential, i.e., virtual, "realities."*

*"What do you say, Honey, shall we have an adventure in Middle Earth tonight, or an hour or two as Scarlet O'Hara and Rhett, or (riffling through the listings) some funky whirls in a black hole, or—heh, heh—perhaps an orgy orchestrated by Bacchus himself?" ("Oh, not that wino again!")*

[*] "A Map Is Not the Territory" is a title that echoes Alfred Korzybski ([1933] 1958, quoted by Eco 1989). This chapter is derived to a large extent from the works of Morris Berman, Yi-Fu Tuan, Timothy Ferris, Wendell Berry, Gregory Bateson, J. Krishnamurti, Jacob Needleman, George Tinker, Jeremy Rifkin, Alan Watts, David Bohm, David Ray Griffin, Arthur Koestler and Simone Weil. The interested reader is directed to their works listed in the References. I gratefully acknowledge my considerable debt to these writers and to the other scholars cited.

August Strindberg, the Swedish playwright and mysogynist, once wrote in his journal: "I hate Woman because she is Earth. I hate Earth because it is me" (quoted by Zeitterling 1989). Such alienation from responsible agency, from personal inwardness and from community with the natural world—the "disease of the West," in Mother Teresa's words (Norwine and Gonzalez 1988) —explains, I believe, our ongoing destruction of that world and perhaps of ourselves, for as Wendell Berry puts it, "a man cannot hate the world and hate his own kind without hating himself" (1970).

Modern alienation generally and the environmental crisis specifically result from a growing isolation of the autonomous modern individual from community, and from a tendency that might be termed a substitution of virtual reality for the virtue of Reality. This is by no means an argument against modern individualism, technology, or freedom. Quintessentially Western and modern, I'm all for the countless technical benefits like personal computers and penicillin, the fruits of an intellectual commitment to reason and a renunciation of superstition. Few of us, I think, would willingly return to a time when a child's sickness was diagnosed and treated as a manifestation of evil spirits. Equally cherished among the legacies of the Western spirit and bound up with its philosophies of art is the tradition of the value of the individual human being.

Notwithstanding all these contributions, however, I find myself surrounded by many and varied evidences of a planetary environmental crisis, perhaps the most salient of which pertain to the illusion of progress. Although since 1950 the world grain production has more than doubled and the total global economic output increased by five times, such progress is illusory, for the gains required the depletion of what Lester Brown terms "natural capital": Earth has lost about one-fifth of its cropland topsoil, one-fifth of its tropical rainforests, and tens of thousands of species (Brown 1990). In addition, the human-enhanced greenhouse effect, acid rain, toxic and hazardous wastes (to say nothing of ordinary garbage), ocean pollution, the loss of wetlands, desertification, air pollution, and the build-up of carcinogens together almost certainly represent the greatest extant threat to the continued well-being and survival of humanity.

What happened? How did we reach such an unfriendly aerie, one from which thoughtful observers agree that by the closing years of the twenty-first century the human community may well have to adjust to a world profoundly debased and diminished by *Homo sapiens*. Our species could even conceivably be extinct by A.D. 2100, having crossed a critical—and unforgiving—threshold, one quite essential to the harmonious operation of "Gaia." An irretrievable mistake.[1]

Intuition, as well as the history of Western science and philosophy, suggests that, along with the naive umbilical cord of superstition, we inadvertently severed another, more vital link with our childhood: a deeply imagistic, profoundly participatory discourse with nature. When we substituted a strictly conceptual dialogue—one which objectified the rest of the cosmos as "Other"—we irrevocably discarded our earlier sense of identification with the natural world. Wendell Berry refers to this loss of naturalness as "the great disaster of human history: the conceptual division between the holy and the world, of Creator from creation" (1970).

This disengagement owes primarily to a handful of distinct changes in the dominant intellectual paradigms of the West, new worldviews which for simplicity I'll label the Judeo-Christian, the Greek, and the mechanical or "Cartesian."[2]

First, certain aspects of both Judaic and Christian traditions have clearly contributed to the progressive "disenchantment" of the world since about 2000 B.C. (of course, the Christian influence has been felt only during the latter half of this period). The Old Testament celebrates the triumph of monotheism over the nature gods of neighboring pagan peoples (Berman 1981), and L. White argues that "in its Western form, Christianity not only established a dualism of man and nature but also insisted that it is God's will that man exploit nature for his proper ends" (1967). Notwithstanding the Christian affinity for the immanent, we find Martin Luther describing the earth as defiled and noxious, the gospel of John forthrightly insisting that neither the world nor the things in it are to be loved, and one modern Christian service insisting that there is "no life, truth, substance nor intelligence in matter" (Ferris 1988). In spite of such iconoclasts as Saint Francis, who tried to substitute for human supremacy the idea of the equality of all creatures (L. White 1967), the dominant Judeo-Christian tenets hold the human being as superior to—and receiver of—the rest of creation, and present earthly life as a sort of trial to be endured rather than enjoyed. These tenets permit, even encourage Christians, as John Stewart Collins has said, to "love God and hate his creations" (Berry 1970).[3]

The second of these great shifts in Western paradigms was the Greek separation of soul from body and in general of subject from object, a "sharp [epistemological] break which occurred sometime between the lifetimes of Homer and Plato" (Berman 1981).[4] The poetic or Homeric mentality, in which the individual learned by emotional identification with the world, was "a life without self-examination, but as a manipulation of the resources of the unconscious in harmony with the conscious, it was unsurpassed" (Havelock 1963). Socrates and Plato regarded this mentality—"participating consciousness," in Berman's phrase—as contemptible, even pathological (Havelock 1963). "The Socratic dictum 'know thyself' posited a deliberately nonsensual type of knowing" (Berman 1981); and Platonism—which ultimately represents "an appeal to substitute a conceptual discourse for an imagistic one" (Havelock 1963)—marked the canonization of the subject/object distinction in the West. As Berman notes, Nietzsche found this Greek rationalism "tragically inverted," for although the creative person works by instinct and checks himself by reason, Socrates did just the reverse (Berman 1981).

Another important metamorphosis in the framework of Western thought occurred in the seventeenth and eighteenth centuries with the abandonment of Aristotelian rationalism—with its emphasis on the metaphysical question *why*—for the empiricisim of the Cartesian-Newtonian "mechanical" worldview—with its more pragmatic central question, *how*. Stephen Toulmin has termed this the "Cartesian division" of matter from mind, causes from reasons, and nature from humanity (1990).[5]

The mechanical paradigm is based in part on the foundational work of several influential thinkers: Francis Bacon, who suggested that the scientific method be based on "objective knowledge," that is, the intellectual separation of people from environment (Rifkin and Howard 1989); Immanuel Kant, who "proved" that humans have no quality of mind which would enable them to intuit the order of nature as it is in itself (Needleman 1970); Adam Smith; and John Locke, who wrote, "the negation of nature is the way toward happiness. People must become effectively emancipated from the bonds of nature" (quoted by Rifkin and Howard 1989).[6]

However, the principal architects of the new worldview were René Descartes, whose mathematical view of nature gave people faith that they could unravel the truths of the world and become its masters; and Sir Isaac Newton, who discovered the mathematical method for describing mechanical motion (Rifkin and Howard 1989), thereby providing the tools with which to put Descartes's paradigm to work.

Modern Western science has, of course, been able to generate a virtual universe of material advances and delights (I for one am unwilling to give up "Masterpiece Theatre," frisbees, and at least the hope of fat-free ice cream), but only because, in Ken Boulding's phrase, *evidence* counts for everything in this paradigm, authority and personal revelation for much less (1980). The Socratic/Baconian legacies of induction, empiricism and logical positivism have together provided an unprepossessing but unrivalled path to the acquisition of information: we plod along, gathering evidence and testing, gathering evidence and testing, rather like squirrels sorting acorns. Yet when you consider the success, or lack thereof, of most other approaches to the mysteries of a human drama played against a cosmic backdrop—politics and economics, say—it is clear that this humdrum but serendipitous methodology represents a human achievement comparable to fire and the wheel. I worry, however, that in keeping our eyes fixed to the path of logic, we forget that the acorns of reason are not only not the only truths, they may not even be the main ones.

The exclusive rationalism of Descartes's mechanical paradigm—a reaction "away from the modest skepticism of the renaissance humanists [such as] Erasmus and Montaigne" (Toulmin 1990)—brought with it a growing presumption that, to quote Rifkin and Howard, "progress is the amassing of greater and greater material abundance, which is assumed to result in an ever more ordered world" (1989).

We now see all around us many legacies of these three great attitudinal shifts, particularly that of the Cartesian "Age of Progress," from a self-definition based on what we own rather than on who we are to the debasement of the planetary ecosystem, which Fletcher eloquently describes in the following passage:

> I found myself looking out over the red fire hydrant and the battered garbage can with its fringe of refuse, looking over and beyond the galvanized chain-link fence, looking through the gross and repulsive spider web of the power pole, with the off-white shape of the hideous gate complex tucked in at the left edge of my vision. And beyond the thick, rolling, ancient panorama of rising, interlocking ridges I saw—spread vividly out before my mind's unhappy eye—our modern panorama of Los Angeles and the Love Canal, Beirut and Chernobyl, Ethiopia and the East Bronx. Beyond them I perceived larger rents that we have torn in the fabric: polluted oceans, raped rainforests, the ozone rift. In that instant of looking I did not need mundane logical bridges to connect those vivid distant vistas with the tattered remnant rags of the saddle in which I stood, or with the paper bag still clutched in my hand and its attendant little pool of ice cream lying white and sticky on the blacktop at my feet. It was a short journey from one to the other, as the canker creeps. (1988)

The Western estrangement in recent centuries between philosophy and the humanities (Toulmin 1990) produced a deep and fundamental commitment—so profound it is a de facto spiritual commitment—to individual, as opposed to group, identity; to control, not empathy; to efficiency and expediency (surely our highest cultural values) rather than to authenticity; to information rather than to discovery; to pleasure rather than to joy; to linear rather than nonlinear time; to knowing rather than understanding; and to becoming rather than to being (Capra 1982). Together, the three great paradigm shifts which occurred in the field of Western thought necessarily led, in Heidegger's phrase, to a forgetfulness of Being: "modern [people], having lost a primeval reverence for nature and having adopted instead a basically instrumental attitude toward the world [and] habituated to thinking instrumentally about nature, tend to think instrumentally about each other as well" (S. Holmes 1988). We got yang but, in getting it, lost yin; we acquired depth in place of surface, and developed the oddest of all sorts of wondering: one lacking wonder. Our attitude became, to paraphrase Descartes, "We think, so we are." The remainder of the Cosmos, being nonsentient, is not us, ergo is not. (Or, restated, "mere matter cannot 'matter.'")[7] Even animals,

Descartes assured us, deserve no more consideration than would the chemicals composing them (Ferre 1988).

So what? you may well ask. If modern reductive materialism works, then as we say in Texas, why fix what ain't broke? In other words, "Why 'postmodernism'?" (Toulmin 1990). Fair questions. The material, moral, social and political successes of the Cartesian paradigm of progress are undeniable. Its direct and indirect contributions to human dignity and welfare in general and to Western art, literature, and music in particular have been enormous. "There is, after all, a close relationship between the West's Faustian spirit and Beethoven's heroic countrapuntal edifices" (Tuan 1989b). Given the obvious fruits of so resoundingly "successful" a model, why then are we not happy with it or, for that matter, with ourselves?[8] The answer is that nonparticipatory consciousness has proved dangerously flawed in a number of fundamental ways.

Long before Hume and Heisenberg, geographers respected and sought the real, knowing too well that, as Korzybski put it, a map is not the territory (1933, quoted by Eco 1989). Now, like many contemporary philosophers and scientists, we have nearly convinced ourselves that a "virtual" map *is* the territory, or at least is its equal.

We began to cut ourselves off from the natural world when, forgetting Korzybski's principle, we came to take the rationalistic knowledge of reductive materialism to be not only the only knowledge but truth itself. ("Materialism" is here at least technically a misnomer, for we don't appear in fact to love or even respect concrete materials [Watts 1970]. As Watts observed, try to find a modern city which looks as though it were made by people who "love material.") A modern biologist, for example, informs us that "man must wake to his total solitude, his fundamental isolation; like a gypsy, he lives on the boundary of an alien world" (Ferre 1988, citing Monod 1972). The angst of such a narrowly positivistic frame of thought owes to its disjunction from actual human experience, which constantly reveals intuitive knowledge all around us. A spider's web, a caterpillar's intricate silken "home," the coral flowers "invented" by flattid bugs (Ferguson 1980) and the migration of butterflies, for example, clearly exhibit a kind of knowledge which is surely not the product of a self-conscious rationality. Moreover, nearly all people regularly enter states of participatory consciousness, those states of awareness in which a connectedness to all other things is felt: consider the loss of self-awareness one experiences during the peak of a musical performance or an anxiety attack, while learning the foxtrot, or having a sexual experience (Berman 1981), or even riding a bike: what began as an almost painfully cognitive process becomes, one day, unselfconscious or "natural."

Human beings also appear commonly to share an intuition that some things—say, the fragile vitality manifest in a two-year-old's nocturnal squalls, the sound of rain on leaves, or a Michael Jordan slam-dunk—are somehow "true" or beautiful, aspects of "reality of the third order" (Koestler 1978), something beyond sensory and conceptual knowledge which has absolute quality—however undefinable and undefendable a proposition that may be (Meadows 1988)—and which are only apprehended through what the Chinese term "no-knowledge" or *wu-wei*. "The heart has its reasons, which Reason does not know" (Pascal [1844] 1952). Pascal's intuitive expression of *wu-wei*, however, hardly gibes with an intellectual paradigm which has "left behind all absolutes, except for absolute faith in our ability to overcome all limits to our physical ability" (Rifkin and Howard 1989).

George Tinker, an Osage Indian and Lutheran theologian, has spoken eloquently of the alienation of modern Western humankind from naturalness:

> The circle marks the wholeness and oneness of all of creation. When Black Elk stood on the top of that ridge looking down on the ravine called Wounded Knee on December 29, 1890, when his heart cried out and tears came down his face and he proclaimed that the Sacred Hoop had been broken, surely he meant the Sacred Hoop of the Ogallala peoples who were being massacred in the ravine below him, the women, the old people, the babies being bayoneted. The balance and harmony of creation was broken, the circle was broken for those people. But surely that's not all Black Elk meant. Spiritually, he's too deep and too rich to see that event affecting only Ogallalas. He meant also to include the bluecoats who were down there perpetrating that atrocity. Surely it was clear to him that the Sacred Hoop had been broken for white people as well as for the Ogallala peoples. And not only broken for two-leggeds alone, but broken for the *grass* that was growing under the bodies that lay there. The Sacred Hoop was broken for the trickle of water that came down the ravine that was now saturated with blood. The Sacred Hoop was broken for all of creation. (Tinker 1988)

As we can obviously never truly "see" nature itself from a mechanistic perspective (but merely the pattern of geometrical forms we project onto it), it is not difficult to recognize how easily we have tended to confuse mathematical analogies of nature with nature itself (Watts 1970). Common sense also informs us that, in practice, the scientist must use intuition for grasping the wholes of nature, hunches which to be useful must be tested "with the thin bright beam of analytic thought" (ibid.). Still, both common-sense observations and intuitive experiences would surely continue to be written off as wishful thinking—after all, positivism insists on the unreality of the unverifiable (the beauty of a crying infant or a rainy wood, for instance) —if it were not that the latest Western scientific revolutions—relativity, "chaos theory" and, especially, quantum physics—inform us, perversely enough, that the nature of mechanical, Cartesian "truth" is, like color or texture, of a fundamentally secondary or derivative quality.

Relativity theory was the first (if oblique) step away from the mechanistic vision toward what has been termed a "field" view (LeShan 1974), for "instead of separate little particles as the constituents of matter, Einstein thought of a field spread through all space, which would have strong and weak regions (or vortices)" (Bohm 1988). A still greater change occurred with quantum theory. According to quantum mechanics, we find that light—being either wavelike or particlelike, depending on the observer's expectation —becomes not exactly either. Matter, too, at least appears to take on an indeterminate, dual quality: quons are potentially (perhaps actually) particles and waves simultaneously, and only "collapse" existentially into one or the other state when observed (King 1989a).[9] David Bohm, from a vantage point well out on the fringes of theoretical physics, states that quantum theory reveals that ultimately no continuous motion exists; that there is an internal relationship between the parts and the whole, and among the various parts, and a context-dependence, as well as an indivisible connection among elements. He sees "the world as one unbroken whole" (Bohm 1988).

The new vision of "chaos theory," too, which examines the nature of nonlinear, dynamical systems, threatens to redefine our fundamental concepts of science and reality, for it "eliminates the Laplacian fantasy of deterministic predictability" (Gleick 1987 quoting an unnamed physicist). Meteorologists, for example, now concede the contingent nature of all long-range weather forecasts, that—to stretch the point—the humble actions of a Chinese butterfly might eventually trigger a thunderstorm in New York. Nonlinear systems sensitive to small perturbations with vastly disproportionate long-run effects seem now to be more normal in nature than exceptional, so that "[to] call the study of chaos 'nonlinear science' was like calling zoology 'the study of nonelephant animals'" (King 1989a).

The most revolutionary new postmodern pattern in the fabric of science—one woven by biologists and social scientists as well as theoretical physicists—raises serious questions about the quantum view itself. Still-speculative studies of the nature of consciousness, for example, are rooted in such pluralistic ground as R. Sperry's split-brain research, the development of general systems theory, Stephen Jay Gould's "punctuated equilibrium" evolution theory, holography, chaos theory, and Ilya Prigogine's so-called "human physics" or theory of dissipative structures, which posits that the very instability and complexity of open systems like living things can perturb the system into newer, "higher" orders of organization (Prigogine and Stengers 1984). These theorists speculatively describe the universe as "intelligent," "holographic" (Pribram 1978; 1979), "implicate" (Bohm 1980; 1988) or "psychosomatic" (Griffin 1988b). According to this view, "perhaps the whole contrast between *mind* and *matter* is the result of a category mistake: trying to compare one thing as known from within, or by identity, with another type of thing known only from without, by nonidentity" (ibid.).

We are now informed that "the idea that human beings can separate themselves from nature, discover its inner secrets, and then use them as a 'fixed body of truths' to manipulate and change the natural world has proven to be [quite] erroneous" (Rifkin and Howard 1989). As physical chemist and 1977 Nobel laureate Ilya Prigogine has said, "instead of the classical description of the world as an automaton, we [must] go back to the Greek paradigm of the world as a work of art" (1972). Max Born, one of the founders of quantum mechanics, has complained that "we have sought for firm ground and found none. The deeper we penetrate, the more restless becomes the universe; all is rushing about and vibrating in a wild dance" (Born 1936 quoted by Rifkin and Howard 1989).

The combination of our alienation from the rest of nature with our unwitting commitment to a flawed scientific paradigm has resulted in the environmental crisis which now threatens to destroy us. In other words, the destruction of our surroundings stems from our having fallen into an ironically circular syllogistic gyre: although we think we know the earth (i.e., as an assemblage of mineral, gaseous, liquid and recently-deceased biological things available for ready conversion into such useful stuff as sausages, toothpaste dispensers, and lawn flamingos), we don't understand it at all and, moreover, at an intuitive level we know that we don't understand.

The Sacred Hoop—our kinship with the natural world—begs for repair. "Our species is now at its most important turning point since the Agricultural Revolution. For the first time humanity has the knowledge to destroy itself quickly, and for the first time humanity also has the knowledge to take its evolution into its own hands and change now, change the way people comprehend and think" (Ornstein and Ehrlich 1989). The question is, as Ruckelshaus puts it, "Can we move nations and people in the direction of sustainability? Such a move would be a modification of society comparable in scale only to the agricultural revolution and the Industrial Revolution. Those revolutions were gradual, spontaneous and largely unconscious. This one will have to be a fully conscious operation" (1989).[10]

If realized, an ecological postmodern worldview would be as different from the Cartesian worldview as Descartes's "scientific heresy" was from the worldview of the Middle Ages (Harman 1988). Whether we are up to the challenge of developing a "sustainability consciousness" (Ruckelshaus 1989) is quite another question. Maybe it's too late for *Homo sapiens* to collectively, in Einstein's words, "dare to be naive" once more. Inexpensive virtual computer systems—no more than a few years away—promise such totally unmediated simulated "personal universes" that actual contact with nature may become as irrelevant as television has rendered the reading of books.

Scientific worldviews, like religious paradigms, are very strongly held commitments and thus enormously resistant to change (Cobb 1988). As Wolf has observed (1990), the world does not change because of conflicts within our ideational culture alone, but by confronting flawed ideas with another paradigm, another ideology, another mindset or *Weltanschauung*. An abstract ideology of environmentalism—"whether fundamentalistic or liberal"

(Boulding 1990)—promises little in the long run. The success of reductive mater-ialism lies not in some abstract ideological strength but in experience, immediate and visceral: "shop till you drop." Therefore, if affirmation of an "ecologicial tautology" (Bateson 1979)—the ecological reinsertion of human beings into the world of natural processes (Toulmin 1990)—is to come, it will require nothing short of a transformation of consciousness through the personal discovery by individual human beings of the pre-Enlightenment *experience* of "tongues in trees, books in the running brooks, sermons in stones, and good in everything" (Shakespeare, *As You Like It*), i.e., an experience realized through an occasional parting of the veil of rationality.[11]

To my individual reader I presume to offer a recommendation: once in a while, surrender that "tyranny of the ego" (P.V.I. Khan 1981), control. How?[12] Firstly, be quiet. Mother Teresa may consider "the disease of the West" to be alienation, but according to Alan Watts it is "excessive verbal communication" (1970). Secondly, pay attention. Notice things. Become aware of that which surrounds you. Pretend that you are a baby just discovering your hands, or a puppy (Japanese haiku often refer to the "Buddha-nature" of puppies and children) trying to investigate the wonders on, say, your family's dining room table by pulling on the tablecloth and discovering, as John Muir put it, that "when we try to pick out anything by itself, we find it hitched to everything else in the universe" (Muir [1912] 1989). As there is no word for what the world is in its natural, nonverbal state, rather than asking, What is it? (which is merely another way of asking, In what class or category is it?), one engages a type of awareness which in Taoism and Zen Buddhism is termed "wordless contemplation" or *kuan* (Watts 1970).

According to Baudelaire, without intellect there is no beauty in nature: it is *all* indirect communication (Abbey 1968; Needleman 1970), requiring and rewarding prolonged participation in much the same way as a Rembrandt or a Picasso (Horn 1989). Note, for example, Martin Buber's instructive contemplation of a single tree:

> Throughout the tree remains my object and has its place and its time span, its kind and condition. But it can also happen, if will and grace are joined, that as I contemplate the tree I am drawn into a relation, and the tree ceases to be an It. The power of exclusiveness has seized me. (1958)

In other words, sometimes consider yourself, like Moses, a "stranger in a strange land," a land whose name is Being. Rebel against "the 'bullying' of the mental stuff that we've received in the course of years and that we take for granted" (P.V.I. Khan 1981). Retreat from the routine that "the mind establishes for its own security and convenience" (Krishnamurti 1990). Try engaging the natural world via a John Muir-like, Taoist alternation between seriously doing nothing—Muir used to tell newcomers to Yosemite to "sit from morning till night under some willow bush on the river bank"—and, well, listen to Muir:

> If for a moment you are inclined to regard [talus slopes] as mere draggled, chaotic dumps, climb to the top of one of them, and run down without any haggling, puttering hesitation, boldly jumping from boulder to boulder with even speed. You will then find your feet playing a tune, and quickly discover the music and poetry of the magnificent rock piles. ([1912] 1989)

If Muir's prescriptions seem excessively intimidating, next week you might—for a more modest first step—try walking or biking to work or around your neighborhood: almost immediately you will experience a palpable, possibly disorienting newness to the landscape, and a sense of being in it as opposed to driving on it.[13] This sensation of the "ultimate basis of intellectual life," as Alfred North Whitehead put it (quoted in Bakko 1989)—of this first-hand knowledge of participatory consciousness—is invariably recognizable by its shocking revelation of a "world, not yet half-made, [which] becomes more beautiful every day" (Muir [1912] 1989). Such experiences catch us unawares, impressing us with the shock of something beyond our control (Tuan 1989a). A pebble on the beach, a bench in the park, one's own hand may seem grotesquely *real* and stubbornly *other* (hence Sartre's "nausea" [1966]) and irreducible to the categories of meaning that we take so much for granted in our rationalizing and mundane lives (Tuan 1972). Edward Abbey refers to this as "the shock of the real":

> A weird, lovely, fantastic object out of nature has the curious ability to remind us—like rock and sunlight and wind and wilderness—that *out there* is a different world, older and greater and deeper by far than ours, a world which surrounds and sustains the little world of men as sea and sky surround a ship. The shock of the real. For a little while we are again able to see, as the child sees, a world of marvels. For a few moments we discover that nothing can be taken for granted, for if this ring of stone is marvelous then all which shaped it is marvelous, and our journey here on earth, able to see and touch and hear in the midst of tangible and mysterious things-in-themselves, is the most strange and daring of all adventures. (Abbey 1968)

If there is a single quality which was once shared even more ubiquitously by scientists, philosophers and theologians than curiosity and a faith that things make sense, it is surely the sense of wonder or awe that such incredible mysteries as, say, Simone Weil's apple (see the epigraph at the beginning of this chapter) actually exist. Wonder, said Goethe, is the highest state that a person can attain (Eckermann 1930). In recent centuries, however, a "squinting extrapolation from the 'success' of scientific method has suffocated our sense of wonder" (Needleman 1970). We continue to seek the celestial mechanics of natural, biological and social systems, forgetting that the predictability of celestial mechanics rests entirely on the singularly

uncharacteristic relative changelessness of a subsystem—our sun and its family
of planets and moons—whose evolution has virtually ceased. This is rather
like predicting human behavior based on the (non)behavior of people in a
cemetery.

If I might be permitted to invoke Simone Weil's apple once more, it
is imperative that we remember that we can know her apple only as it is in
our minds, never as it truly is. There is another comprehension, however: that
of simplicity. Simplicity becomes accessible when we penetrate into the sheer
wonder of being, when we are willing, in William Blake's famous phrase, "To
see a World in a Grain of Sand" ("Auguries of Innocence").

"What is this life if, full of care, we have no time to stand and stare?"
asked William Henry Davies. "Standing and staring" is what T. N. Hanh
describes as entering something rather than standing outside of it, a
"penetrating awareness" (1987). For two millennia and more, Greek and later
Western scholars have striven to stand far above their material, for a "view
from nowhere" (Nagel 1986; Tuan 1989a) or, as Descartes and Laplace would
have it, as "rational onlookers." We can no longer view the world this way.
"Our place is within the same world that we are studying, and whatever
scientific understanding we achieve must be a kind of understanding that is
available to participants within the processes of nature or from within"
(Toulmin 1982). It has become clear that "when we want to understand
something, we cannot just stand outside and observe it. We have to enter
deeply into it and be one with it in order really to understand. To
'comprehend' something means literally to pick it up and be one with it.
There is no other way to understand something" (Hanh 1987). Ninety years
ago, William James observed,

> It is absurd for science to say that the egotistic elements of experience should be
> suppressed. The axis of reality runs solely through the egotistic places—they are
> strung upon it like so many beads. A concrete bit of personal experience may be a
> small bit, but it is not a mere abstract element of experience, such as the "object" is
> when taken all alone. It is a *full* fact, even if insignificant and it is the *kind* to which
> all realities whatsoever must belong. ([1902] 1958)

In other words, although there seems to be no route back to the
"naturalness" of a simple nature mysticism, further understanding requires a
softening of the divide between analysis and the *esprit de finesse*, as Pascal put
it (Barzun 1989)—the old intuitive road to the "pure frequency domain"
(Pribram 1982), participatory consciousness. We can, after all, see an
individual leaf in all its clarity without losing sight of its relation to the tree
(Watts 1970). Postmodern science, Ferre states, must keep "the modern tools
of analysis sharp in their proper role as tools and send us back into the
Garden to work with respect and caution" (1988).

In 1970, J. Krishnamurti—himself already a septuagenarian—reminded a group of college students of the toddler's natural gift of artless simplicity:

> I don't know if any of you have noticed, early in the morning, the sunlight on the waters. How extraordinarily soft is the light, and how the dark waters dance, with the morning star over the trees, the only star in the sky. Do you even notice any of that? Or are you so busy, so occupied with the daily routine, that you forget or have never known the rich beauty of this earth—this earth on which all of us have to live? (1970)

The true definition of science is this: the study of the beauty of the world. "Heaven's net is vast," says Lao-tsu, "its meshes are wide; yet nothing gets through" (quoted by Weil 1952). On his deathbed, Goethe's final words were "mehr licht!" (more light!) (R. Miller 1989). Facing infinite ignorance and armed only with finite knowledge, we must nevertheless struggle toward that light which is Truth, i.e., that which is, in the words of the Christian mystic Meister Eckhart, "something so noble that if God could turn aside from it, I could keep to the truth and let God go" (quoted by Blakney 1941).

Truth, Krishnamurti repeatedly advises, is a pathless land (1989), but his advice to notice, feel and even love the earth suggests that the natural world of ephemeral but real daffodils (for example) does offer a kind of touchstone with the direction in which Truth lies. Although neglected and nearly forgotten, the significance of this benchmark—the earth or nature—is absolutely real, and "we are obliged by the fact of our utter dependence on it to listen more closely than we have to its messages" (Ruckelshaus 1989).[14]

A doppelgänger lies at the end of the tunnel of rationality, one whose shadow—in the form of the environmental crisis, among other things—warns that, just as the way back to innocent ignorance is forever sealed and guarded by "an angel with a shining sword" (Boulding 1980), mankind is now "like a lame man of good vision who needs a blind man of sure foot" (Ralston 1979). The myth of Antaeus turns out to be true: humankind is a formidable wrestler but loses strength when both feet are not planted on Mother Earth (ibid.). The analytic measurement of nature tells us nothing if we cannot see nature in any other way (Watts 1970).[15] In the words of the 2,300-year-old Samkhya sutra, we must seek understanding down a path where merge *purusa* (spirit) and *prakrti* (Nature) (Radhakrishnan and Moore 1957).

In physics, the principle of complementarity suggests that different, even contradictory explanations of some phenomena may be equally valid.[16] The postmodern "heresy" promises to be that of a fundamentally *complementary* science (Sperry 1981, 1987; Popper and Eccles 1984; Harman 1988).[17] Spencer's 1904 admonition (cited in Durant 1961) that truth generally lies in a reconciliation of antagonistic opinions seems to me never more appropriate than at the present, when—among the rational, religious and "scientific" paradigms—no *one* can any longer be naively assumed to be correct.

The world is almost certain to become increasingly placeless, thingless: "virtual." The impact of computers, primitive virtual devices, and today's computer networks together is analagous to that of "wireless" communication early in this century, or better, of the first few books to roll off Gutenberg's press. The hyperworld of the twenty-first century will be dazzling, almost literally enchanting. Possibly, though, it may also further trivialize our experience of the real (e.g., a virtual kiss) and thus further distance us from the mystery of truth.

Should we choose to turn away from an inclusive, syncretic, truly postmodern ecological worldview to any narrow perspective, either that of scientism or that of a new pantheism, I fear we will soon collectively discover that, as Antoine de Saint-Exupéry worried,

> nobody grasped us by the shoulder while there was still time. Now the clay of which we were shaped has dried and hardened, and naught in us will ever awaken the sleeping musician, the poet, the astronomer that possibly inhabited us in the beginning. (Quoted by Rowell 1986)

Dying without having fully lived might well be an unforgivable sin. Aborting Gaia—that is, prematurely carrying Earth back into the void—would surely be another.

## Notes

1.  "From a biologist's perspective the outcome is not surprising. Despite the logic and reason that show long-term disaster, humans go for short-term benefit as they are programmed genetically to do, as individuals of any species are programmed. In this case, sane use of resources goes against millions of years of evolutionary wisdom which dictates 'sequester and reproduce'" (Rappole 1989).

2.  This treatment of the development of a mechanistic paradigm is necessarily limited and relatively superficial. The interested reader is directed to the recent book edited by David Ray Griffin (1988) listed among the References.

3.  Pope John Paul II devoted his January 1, 1990, message for the annual World Day of Peace to a plea for mankind to protect and preserve creation for future generations; it was the first papal document dedicated exclusively to ecology. Citing the book of Genesis, the pope pointed out that God saw the world as good and that Nature and human beings were then in harmony. The devastation of the world of nature "results from the behavior of people who show a callous disregard for the hidden, yet perceivable requirements of the order and harmony which govern nature itself." His Holiness' intent is admirable, and I hope that his message saves some topsoil or birds. In the long run, however, do we not treasure that which we love, and love that with which we identify? Meaningful reconciliation between *Homo sapiens* and (the rest of) "nature" seems unlikely to me so long as we retain a

fundamentally dualistic (I-It) perspective of our place in the scheme of things. I concede, however, the impressive and growing importance of American and European "green" ecopolitical movements. Perhaps a dualistic but pragmatic cart can precede a holistic horse. I hope so.

4.    An object/subject dichotomy appeared early in some Eastern traditions as well, such as the "rational" Nyaya Hindu orthodox system of around 200 B.C. Moreover, as Gould has noted, the sharpness of the break between Homer and Plato is arguable: the Babylonian maps of 4000 B.C. and even the maps scratched on mammoth bones along the Dnepr River c.15,000 B.C. clearly seem to be "objectifying representations of the world," or separating subject from object (Gould 1990).

5.    Obviously, other great thinkers made key contributions to the development of what I have termed the "mechanistic paradigm." Among the more important of these contributions was Comte's positivism. Those interested are directed to the various summary treatments of his work, as well as those of the work of Rousseau, Kant, Hegel, Schopenhauer, Berkeley, Pascal, Hume, Spinoza, William James, Nietzsche, Darwin, Spencer and, of course, Bacon and Descartes, which appear in the compendia by Commins & Linscott (1954) and by Durant (1961), listed among the References. Concerning the schism between *why* and *how*, Darwin's biological evolution and Spenser's universal evolution did help to tie these questions together (*see* Durant 1961).

6.    However, "Locke may well have meant something quite different by the statement 'the negation of nature is the way towards happiness' than we might mean today" (Gould 1990).

7.    Perhaps even more appealing is the old, humble wisecrack: "What is Matter? Never Mind! What is Mind? No Matter!" (Toulmin 1990).

8.    There is much to admire in postmodern Western society. I think not only, or even particularly, of the material advances, terrific as they are, but of an attitude of openness and a growing spirit of acceptance of difference and of uncertainty. However, the undeniable greed and fear which pulse through our lives are deeply disturbing.

9.    A point worth contemplating is the argument by Mortimer Adler and others that it remains possible (probable, Adler would say) that quantum physicists are the latest in a long line of gifted thinkers to be guilty of the "idealist error." Subatomic reality *seems* to be intrinsically indeterminate but that indeterminacy could yet be an effect of "the intrusive and disturbing measurement of those objects and events" (Adler 1990). From another standpoint, Hegel's perhaps, our present understanding of the role and centrality of each individual observer is merely one more step in the ongoing unfolding of Reason or God.

10.    It may be argued that Ruckelshaus's opinion that humanity "has the knowledge to take its evolution into its own hands" is just more positivistic hubris. For example, Ian King states, "I would claim that a truly 'ecological consciousness' readily admits to imperfect knowledge and that the practical application of any 'human knowledge' is fraught with unintended consequences and unforeseen complications" (1989b).

11.    However, Milbrath (1989) argues impressively that it may be possible for us to "learn our way out" of our present dilemma (including the environmental crisis) to a "sustainable" society.

12.  Most of this chapter is an attempt to trace the ways Cartesian/mechanistic thinking came to dominate the modern Western world, and the legacy of this paradigm vis-à-vis the "environmental crisis." This argument recalls that of Rousseau, perhaps, but I do not believe that humankind is "bad" and Nature "good" (Rousseau [1781] 1945); rather, I suggest that our unhappiness—and such manifestations thereof as the "environmental crisis" —originates in our conscious and unnecessary estrangement from (the rest of) nature and, thereby, from the harmony of naturalness.  It may, of course, be argued that rationality per se has not been the culprit but "the wrong premises from which reason draws faulty conclusions" (Griffin 1990).  I leave it to the reader to decide whether our most fundamental understandings are, paraphrasing Boulding, "based on an internal operation on the part of the mind or a 'visitation' into the mind from a reality beyond the senses" (Boulding 1990).  My own pathetic experience with *wu-wei* points toward the latter.

13.  Through such mundane "meditation," the goal of a "felt shift" (Ferguson 1980) or what the Buddhists term "satori"—sudden insight—becomes possible; beware, however, of straining or "trying" for awakening, for that won't work.  Incidentally, any reader too tired, rational, sedentary or simply curmudgeonly to walk or bike could try listening attentively to, say, Beethoven's Ninth Symphony, Ho-Chan Hao's "The Butterfly Lovers" or Ralph Vaughn Williams' "The Lark Ascending," all of which can help to distract one from self-conscious rationality.

14.  See also I. King's undated paper, "Political Economy and the 'Laws of Beauty': Aesthetics, Economics and Materialism in the Thought of Karl Marx."

15.  Nor are we informed, I think, by any new pantheism ("deep ecology"?) which values *only* the whole, as opposed to the whole and, equally, the individual.

16.  "Let science admit that its 'laws' apply only to phenomena and the relative; let religion admit that its theology is a rationalizing myth for a belief that defies conception. . . . Let science cease to deny deity, or to take materialism for granted.  Mind and matter are, equally, relative phenomena, the double effect of an ultimate cause whose nature must remain unknown" (H. Spencer quoted by Durant 1961).

17.  Stephen Toulmin—paraphrasing Gerald Holton—reminds us that "Neils Bohr grew up in a household where Kierkegaard's ideas about 'complementary' modes of thought were discussed at Sunday dinner" (Toulmin 1990).

## Review and Reflections on the Text

1.    Define aerie; paradigm; *Weltanschauung*; positivism; Gaia; *wu-wei*; *kuan*; syncretic.

2.    What does it mean to describe something as "other"?

3.  What is it that Mother Teresa calls the "disease of the West"? Can you think of any examples within your own experience which illustrate its debilitating potential?

4.  What is meant by the phrase "a deeply imagistic, profoundly participatory discourse with nature"? Have you ever had an experience or heard or read of experiences that could be described in this way? If so, what was their context and what was their significance to the participants?

5.  Make a brief outline of the major changes in worldview that the author associates with the Judeo-Christian, the Greek, and the Cartesian worldviews.

6.  What are the advantages of induction, empiricism, and logical positivism? What are their disadvantages?

7.  List some examples of intuitive knowledge other than those cited by the author.

8.  List some activities in which you have experienced a state of unselfconscious participatory consciousness other than those mentioned by the author.

9.  Name one or two experiences you recall as having an "absolute quality" beyond rational explanation. Can you explain what makes them unexplainable?

10.  Try writing a few lines of prose or poetry to express what you understand by the Sacred Hoop whose rupture Black Elk lamented. Can you transpose Tinker's explanation of the historical and natural elements of the Sacred Hoop into a modern, urban setting?

11.  In what respects do relativity theory, quantum mechanics, and chaos theory modify the mechanical paradigm?

12.  Respond to Prigogine's suggestion that we need to recover "the Greek paradigm of the world as a work of art."

13.  What in the author's view is the root cause of the current ecological crisis? Do you agree? Why or why not?

14.  Speculate about some of the elements of a "sustainability consciousness" such as Ruckelshaus advocates. What kinds of awareness, behaviors, and values would it require?

15. Explain how "excessive verbal communication" might interfere with understanding.

16. Some suggested *kuan* exercises: (1) At dawn or twilight, spend twenty or thirty relaxed minutes alone in your backyard or a nearby park, simply absorbing and savoring sensations of sight, sound, touch, and smell as they present themselves to you, without identifying, describing, or evaluating anything. Later, draw a picture or write a few lines about what you experienced. Consider the differences and similarities between your experience and your rendering of it. (2) Walk or bike along a route you usually travel in a car, bus, train or streetcar. List a few things you notice which you have not noticed before. Do any of them strike you as in some way truly meaningful or important, or are all these new observations merely trivial?

17. Think about instrumental (i.e., nonvocal) music you have enjoyed. While listening, have you ever found yourself experiencing the "pure frequency domain"? If so, how did you recognize it? How would you describe the feeling to someone else?

18. Can you recall any moment when you have felt what Abbey calls "the shock of the real"? Describe this moment as best you can, what seemed to provoke it, and how you felt about it.

19. Reflect in writing on the title of this chapter. For example, what is the meaning and significance of the phrase, "a map is not the territory"? Why do you suppose that the author is concerned about the likely coming effects of new technologies such as "virtual reality"?

20. What do you think about this: If virtual reality is great fun and very useful—and it will be both—and feels as real as real, if a virtual kiss, for example, seems at the moment the same experience as an actual smooch by an actual other person, won't that be just as good as reality, or in fact better, because real people sometimes have dandruff and halitosis and may decide not even to kiss us. . . ?

# III. Geographer's Quest

Out beyond ideas of right doing and wrong doing there is a field. I'll meet you there.
                                          —Jalal Al-Din Rumi, thirteenth-century Persian poet

Since the middle of this century, North American academic geographers have adopted an almost exclusively pragmatic and "scientific" (objective, empirical, numerical and, especially, positivist) vision of their discipline. The gains won by this approach have been beyond either question or measure. For example, in my own research specialty, climatology, the combined impacts of the statistical, computer and remote sensing "revolutions" have been nothing short of transformative.

The costs attendant to this paradigm-shift have also proved high, if largely unnoticed. With respect to the negative feedback loop which can be created by a discipline's narrowly defining itself on strictly pragmatic grounds, one need only consider the present predicament of academic geology in American universities. Geography, too, risks becoming paradoxically "hyper-real and unreal when it strives to be most prosaic, when it sticks to factual minutiae and is loaded with a surfeit of place-name and statistical information" (Tuan 1990b).

I am, however, here more interested in the effects of a generation of "scientism" on scholarship in contemporary American geography. Three such consequences are I think particularly worrisome.

Firstly, although it has been evident for at least a generation that a simple-minded, pre-quantum "Cartesian" or mechanistic scientific paradigm is passé, clearly we—and many other social scientists—have not yet caught on.

> Relativity eliminated the Newtonian illusion of absolute space and time; quantum theory eliminated the Newtonian dream of a controlled measurement process; and chaos eliminates the Laplacian fantasy of deterministic predictability. (Gleick 1987, quoting an unnamed physicist)

Nobel laureate Ilya Prigogine has pointed out that randomness and irreversibility play an ever-increasing role at all scales (1972). A great deal of our work, however, suggests that we are still laboring under the ponderously naive supposition that nature is fundamentally stable, orderly and, therefore, predictable. As I've developed this theme more fully in the preceding chapter, I shan't belabor it here but merely note that whatever its status in the minor subsystem called geography, "exceptionalism" is very much alive and well in the universe at large.

Secondly, we geographers have unnecessarily marginalized ourselves by foregoing our traditional kinship with the humanities. The central question of the humanities—What is it to be human?—appears more vital than ever in an era whose anthems seem to be narcissism, solipsism, and that "particular anxiety of the stranger" (O'Rourke 1988), anomie. "Personal human experience has become much more intricate than it was two generations ago at the dawn of quantum physics" (Stuart 1990). Which of us is such a Pollyanna as to be able to read of the record homicide rates in 1990 in New York City, Houston and Chicago without a tremulous recognition of what Baudelaire, in his prophecy of universal "progress" (or ruin), called "the debasement of our souls" (quoted by Paz 1989)?[1]

> This summer, in one eight-day period, four children [in New York City] were killed by stray gunshots as they played on the sidewalks, toddled in their grandmother's kitchens or slept soundly in their own beds. So many have died that a new slang term has been coined to describe them: "mushrooms," as vulnerable as tiny plants that spring up underfoot. ("Decline of New York" 1990)

Who among us can watch, along with fifty others (mainly children), a rerun of "Miami Vice" or "Dallas" on a remote village's new television set without experiencing a shudder of fear that our postmodern gift to the Third World is the ability to pass virtually overnight from "tribalism to decadence" (Will 1990)?

Too few American geographers are addressing these themes today. Is it realistic to expect to fathom the nature and direction of the changing human geographies of, say, East Asia or the Middle East if we lack a working grasp of the philosophies and ethical codes of conduct of the Judeo-Graeco-Roman "root," much less the teachings of the traditional wisdom-systems of India, China and Japan (Howard 1985)? I think not.

A few years ago I experienced a dark moment of despair when, while attending the annual meeting of the Association of American Geographers in

Toronto, I listened to paper after paper which "analyzed" the overarching, unfolding patterns of human geography—e.g., the collapse of state socialism, Europe 1992, the Islamic "alternative," and the eerily pyrrhic "victory" of the West—by simply rearranging economic and ideological schemata. The most glaring problem with this approach, beside the inherent shortcomings of any positivistic analysis of questions of value or "quality" (see point three, below), is that political and economic matters are derivative, that is, on the *secondary* level of human thinking. "Social and political conditions in the several areas of the world depend, in the final analysis, upon the philosophical and spiritual thought and ideals" (Radhakrishnan and Moore 1957), and on the reasoning and emotions, of the peoples of the world.

In Toronto, I waited in vain for appropriate references to lessons bequeathed by either the "elite" or the "traditional" spiritual and philosophical systems. Surely a comprehension of the leitmotif of the age—the convergence of traditional certainties with modern self-awareness, and their consequent metamorphosis into ad hoc postmodernism—lies to a great extent in poets, mystics and thinkers like Black Elk and Plato, Yeats and Achebe, and Spengler and Simone Weil (for example). How else to comprehend a world in which "the assertion of the popular will [has made] mutual understanding between peoples *more* difficult, not *less*" (Howard 1985, my emphasis), and where the victory of Western liberal democracy—the so-called "end of history" (Fukuyama 1989)—has given us a new, multipolar, post-Cold War world which is proving to be, to quote Mearsheimer, "a design for tension, crisis and possibly even war" (1990, quoted by Geyer 1990)?[2]

Octavio Paz has written of the importance of the *other* voice, "the voice of silence and of tumult, mad wisdom and wise madness, the intimate murmur in the bedroom and the surging crowd in the square" (1989). "Poets nourished the thought of Hobbes and Locke, Marx and Tocqueville" (ibid.). Such few contemporary sages as we have, like Vaclav Havel and Andrei Sakharov—exemplars of action *and* thought—were not born of vacuous ordinariness but were "nourished by Shakespeare, Goethe, Dickens, Swift, Mark Twain, Tolstoy, Gogol and Pushkin" (Maddocks 1990).

As Melvin Maddocks has observed, this kind of generalized anti-intellectualism has left Americans "looking for the first time old-fashioned, tired, in need of. . . what? Ideas?" (Maddocks 1990). How painfully ironic is this state of affairs, for it is just now, when we are "finally relieved of the struggle against totalitarian superstition," in Octavio Paz's optimistic phrase, that we "should be reflecting on the deficiencies and lacunae of the principles on which liberal democracy are based" and, finally, on "the questions we humans ask about fraternity, about origins and final ends, about the meaning and the value of existence" (Paz 1989). These are the themes of humanitarian thinkers past and present, and through them geographers can tap the images that connect what we study with why we study it.

The third and last but most troublesome consequence of "scientific" geography is our abandonment of the literary tradition in American professional geography. "Academic geographers have eschewed the view from *somewhere*: landscapes with horizons that evoke a sense of goal and of adventure do not seem to exist for them except in the letters they write home" (Tuan 1990b, my emphasis). This particular failure of nerve—the most grievous scholarly sin of my generation, I think—must not be blamed on the so-called quantitative revolution. I've thoroughly enjoyed my own long-standing dalliance with empiricism, induction, and those irreplaceable "figments of the human imagination" (Boulding 1980), numbers. Along the line, though, enchanted by these useful if elaborate "glimpses of the obvious" (ibid.), we lost the will or courage or perhaps simply the inclination to pursue less rationalistic corridors to spatial questions. (Not, however, the *ability* to do so, as Peter Haggett's recent book, *The Geographer's Art* [1990], makes abundantly clear, as does Lowenthal's *The Past is a Foreign Country* [1986] and Symanski's *Outback Rambling* [1990].)

Let us recall once again Picasso's proposition that art is the lie which teaches the truth—an illusion, to paraphrase a remark Robinson Jeffers wrote somewhere, which tricks mankind beyond our limits. Joseph Campbell described such intuitions and revelations as "fictions through which insight into the depths of being is conveyed anagogically" (1972). In John Berger's words, art is "an organized response to what Nature allows us to glimpse occasionally. Art sets out to transform the potential recognition into an unceasing one" (1986).

In his recent seminal work, George Steiner makes an extraordinary case for what he terms "real presences" (1989). Artistic intuition may be our only entrée to such presences. Science, the orderly detection of error (Boulding 1980), is our most marvelous means of learning about Truth but can by definition never teach Truth. We cannot have a "science of nature," as Heisenberg and Thompson have reminded us, only a science of human knowledge about nature (Stuart 1990 citing Thompson 1987). Ignorance is infinite, knowledge terribly finite (a thought original with philosopher of science Karl Popper; *see* Popper 1975). Compare, for instance, the innocent single-mindedness of a numerical model like a General Circulation Model with the incredible complexity—and, more significantly, the awful reality—of the natural system it endeavors to imitate.

Art is that prosthetic lens of intuition which somehow enhances the brain's function of protecting us "from being overwhelmed and confused by this mass of largely useless and irrelevant knowledge" (Campbell 1972). In this way, the metaphors and images of art "give *meanings*" (ibid.) and reveal *relationships* which offer entrée to the geographer's raison d'être, the pattern. Speaking on the human capacity to comprehend the universe mathematically, Werner Heisenberg suggested that "patterns in our minds" may "reflect the internal structure of the world" in ways mathematics cannot (1970, quoted by Laing 1976).[3] "Whatever the explanation of these other forms of understanding may be, the language of the images, metaphors and similes, is probably the only way to approach the 'one' from wider regions" (ibid.). Surely this is what Baudelaire meant when he said that poets are the universal translators, because they translate the language of the universe, stars, water and trees into the language of humans (quoted by Paz 1989).

In history, the tradition of scholar-as-artist is alive, if not exactly well, as evidenced by the considerable popular success of Barbara Tuchman's books. In literature, biography and travel writing are vital, and both of these must inevitably be in large measure interpretive fictions. And, in the physical and biological sciences, of all places, we have in recent years witnessed a virtual literary flood.[4]

Does not, you may well inquire, the speculative, subjective, often idiosyncratic work of the likes of Prigogine, Bohm, Bateson, Ferris, Pribram and Sperry ramble at times far off the path to understanding? Perhaps, but an equally fair question is, *what* path? Truth is forever "aporia" (Gould 1990)—Krishnamurti's pathless land—discoverable only "through understanding the contents of [one's] own mind, through observation and not through intellectual analysis or introspective dissection" (Krishnamurti 1990).[5] As we are all groping and extemporizing our way toward what we can only hope is the source from which the light of reason is kindled, as Saint Augustine put it, even disoriented shouts out of the mist offer useful perspective.

In the meantime, American academic geographers left these risky, subjective heights for the safer playing fields of objectivism.

> Even when geographers study a particular place, they tend to describe and understand it from an impersonal standpoint. Humans become abstractions and cannot engage in any quest other than the economic, with the inevitable consequence that their material environment too is drained of a great deal of substantiality and meaning. (Tuan 1990b)

In discarding the potentially frivolous for the merely mundane, we contributed to one of the more frightening impulses of the age, a trivialization of interests.[6] If truth is, as Heidegger claimed, "unconcealment," we do well to worry about pursuit of the trivial, for in the shadowy forests of trivia, truth, as Gould says, "can go back into concealment":

> You may remember that Anaximander said the earth and the other planets go around the sun, but then Ptolemy said whatever the Greek equivalent is of "balderdash," or even something worse, and for two thousand years the western world believed the sun went around the earth. (1990)

A geographer's quest requires reading patterns as well as "unconcealing" them. Our most ambitious, difficult and worthy question is, so what? Like it or not, the scholarly heirs of Anaximander are impelled to seek the conjunction of truth with meaning if only because, in Giordano Bruno's words, "out of the world we cannot fall" (quoted by LeShan 1974). Such a reconciliation can only be effected by a humane postmodern geography which, like the other postmodern sciences (e.g., ecology and quantum physics), is rooted in Bohr's and Kierkegaard's complementarity of intuition and rationality (Toulmin 1990). That is, to paraphrase Paz, a reconciliation built on the suspension bridge between science and art (Maddocks 1990) or, to borrow Yeats's metaphor, between image and book.

Finally, my argument here has been that while analysis should perhaps predominate in geography, some degree of "invention" or artistry is essential to the vitality of so synthetic an academic discipline. If, as seems reasonable, the values professed by a professor resonate in the written work of that academic's best students, I suggest that academic geographers examine carefully such work as a guide to the scholarly qualities they are, and are not, encouraging. In other words, if one's finest students are consistently writing solidly substantive essays which lack any spark of poetry, a reassessment of fundamental pedagogic assumptions (e.g., regarding what is important and appropriate in advanced geography courses) is respectfully recommended.

Recently, I asked my students in a junior-level Oriental Philosophy class (teaching duties can be remarkably varied at small regional universities!) to respond in a few hundred to a few thousand words to part or all of the Vedas, the oldest Hindu hymns. The following essay, written by a sophomore chemistry major, beautifully exemplifies the pedagogic value of a marriage of "analysis" and "invention," and is therefore presented verbatim:

### Hymn of Creation

(A modernized version of the Vedic "Hymn of Creation,"
based loosely on modern scientific principles.)

#### By Ricardo Delgado

"Que la terre est petite à qui la voit des cieux." [How small is the earth to one who sees it from the heavens.]

In the Beginning there was Potential. It was both insignificant and infinite.
There were no points of reference and nothing was relative to anything else.
Where was this Potential? The question is Unanswerable and the answer Illogical.
What was this Potential? The Potential was the Ultimate.
When did this occur? Both an Eternity and a breath ago.

There existed no dark mysterious chill of Night or light, powerful warmth of day.

There was no Chaos and no Order.

Then there came an appalling spark in the depths of this infinite calm.

Was this spark Conflict, Desire, Heat, or Force of Will? It was beyond words, we cannot say. It was beyond the parameters of good or evil; beyond light and dark.

The spark gave reference and relativity.

The spark gave Time.

And in that instant the spark foretold of the Great Pattern of things to come. It spoke of the great energy of the nuclear fires, and the tempest of the Elemental and Stellar Winds. It spoke of the Scientists and Wizards; the Medicine Men and Prophets, who would contemplate its myriad facets and intricacies.

Power and Creativity were born of the Potential, and nourished one another. Energy begat Matter and Matter begat Energy.

What governed the course of the Great Pattern? Who can say?

Intrinsic to the Pattern were Order and Chaos. Out of Order were born the Laws. But they were born after Time began its unceasing march, and cannot know the Beginning; cannot know the spark.

Out of Chaos too was born a Law. The Law of Chaos was devious, spiteful, and envious. The Law of Chaos, Destroyer of Order, unrelentingly demanded homage from the Laws of Order and became Entropy.

But even Entropy does not know the Beginning. Neither the Laws of Order nor the Law of Chaos can know all of, or change, the Great Pattern.

And perhaps even Order and Chaos may only guess at the End.

Geography is about images of places—maps—but, to paraphrase Hume, we can never know how closely our mental images approximate Truth. "A map is not the territory" (Korzybski 1933 quoted in Eco 1989); nor is a Geographic Information System, a statistical model, or a differential equation. As Yi-Fu Tuan suggested recently (1990b), geography is not merely "basic knowledge" or information but also an imaginative project effected through images, metaphors and similies; in other words, through the art of geography.

## Notes

1.    I suggest that any professor who doubts this consider the decline of civility in that peculiar but instructive social subsystem, the university classroom.

2.    While the recent Liberian and Sri Lankan experiences—"brutal civil wars irrelevant to the rest of the world," in Georgie Anne Geyer's cruel and somewhat hyperbolic phrase (1990)—were more than sufficiently unpleasant, the ongoing tragic cases of Peru, Yugoslavia and Kashmir seem to me more worrying because they suggest that postmodern tribal, ethnic, national and religious passions can be as mindless as ever and, potentially, even more destructive.

3.    Life, the universe, and existence itself are, it can hardly be stressed too much, mysterious beyond words. For any geographers who do *not* occasionally experience an awed, silenced

wonder at the nature of Nature—e.g., that it *is*, makes sense, and is in some degree fathomable—alternative forms of employment are recommended. In other words, because we pursue the sublime with mundane (but effective) methods in no way renders the sublime itself mundane.

4. Even mathematicians are getting into the act. A colleague informed me recently that his calculus students, together with beginning calculus students at various American universities, are learning by writing weekly imaginative essays!

5. The complete extract from Krishnamurti is well worth recollection:

> Truth is a pathless land. Man cannot come to it through any organization, through any creed, through any dogma, priest or ritual, not through any philosophic knowledge or psychological technique. He has to find it through the mirror of relationship, through the understanding of the contents of his own mind, through observation and not through intellectual analysis or introspective dissection. (1990)

6. Writing, Graham Greene has said, is a form of therapy: "Sometimes I wonder how all those who do not write, compose or paint can manage to escape the madness, the melancholia, the panic fear which is inherent in the human situation" (quoted by Storr 1988). Is not the fact that we do not *require* such "therapy" an indictment of our trivialization of the interplay of humankind and Earth?

## Review and Reflections on the Text

1. Define narcissism; solipsism; anomie; aporia.

2. Briefly summarize the three "worrisome" consequences of scientism in current American scholarship in geography.

3. Explain what the author means by his assertion that "political and economic matters are derivative, that is, on the *secondary* level of human thinking."

4. To what extent do you feel that familiarity with the spiritual and philosophical roots of a people is significant to geographical studies? Explain your answer.

5. Of what use are the arts, or artistic intuitions, to scientists in general, geographers more particularly, and you most specifically?

6. How can pursuit of the trivial cause or contribute to the concealment of truth?

7.   The author mentions Popper's observations that "ignorance is infinite" while "knowledge is terribly finite," and Heidegger's claim that truth is "unconcealment." How are these two thoughts related?

8.   What does the author mean when he says that geographers *read* patterns?

# IV. Postmodern American PopMyths

I felt like a man who, having vaguely thought that all flowers are much the same, goes for a walk with a botanist.

—Iris Murdoch, *Under the Net*

American scholars have in recent decades tended to denigrate (or worse yet, been ignorant of) the influences of philosophical and theological worldviews on cultural patterns and human ecologies. Regardless of academic ephemera, however, the values, attitudes, and behaviors of world cultures remain in very large measure a product of *Weltanschauung* (worldview) and *Zeitgeist* (the spirit of the times), which in turn reflect a collectivity of philosophical, spiritual, scientific and emotional assumptions or "truths" (a theme more fully addressed in Chapter V). This is not to claim that humans are automatons. They are complex and conscious creatures very ready to defy their cultural (and other forms of) "programming." This is the root of their unpredictability and fascination. Still, by studying a culture's fundamental assumptions about the nature of the good life, one may begin to access its "realities" and, therefore, the culture itself.[1]

It is a truism that until the last century or so, much of Western philosophy represented a ceaseless dialectic between the differing "realities" of Platonism and Aristotelianism: ideal, transcendent and universal (forms or ideas) versus the empirical and particular (things). Both elite *and* traditional Western attitudes, values and behaviors still to some extent reflect the tension between these and later but related antinomies (e.g., Kant and Sartre). Increasingly, however, popular and scholarly sensibilities alike reveal a postmodern, almost postexistential suspicion that "anything goes." The new shared assumption regarding the fundamental nature of reality, truth and, therefore, meaning is that because nature is uncertain, contingent and fuzzy, absolutes (like Truth) are absolutely absent. (The concession that an inaccessible "divine" or Other language or realm may exist begs the vital question of whether or not one acts as though it does. Refer to the discussion of Confucius in the next chapter.) Questions of ideal-versus-particular or essence-against-existence presuppose some manner of ultimate. Little surprise that "anything goes" when all of existence save the contingent fluxes of relation has become as chimerical as the Ghost of Christmas Past. There are, we are informed, only socially created realities. Not long ago, essayist Lewis Thomas responded:

> We like to tell each other these days, in our hubris, that we are the thinking part, the earth's awareness of itself; without us and our marvelous brains, even the universe would not exist—we form it and all the particles of its structure, and without us on the scene the whole affair would pop off in the old random disorder. I believe only a little of this. (1990)

Twenty years ago H. E. Daly (1973) proposed a simple, pyramid-shaped diagram of human values. His "quality triangle" schematized a modern worldview which reconciled the classic and the traditional. Broadly speaking, neither Socrates nor Black Elk would have argued with his "ultimate ends" of the good human life: harmony, fulfillment, identity, security, creativity, happiness, community, and enlightenment; beauty and justice are understood as by-products of devotion to, quest for, and service to these ends. Freedom is good because, like health, it is not only a desirable intermediate end but more importantly is a requisite means to the ultimate ends.

The gathering *Weltanshauung* of postmodern America demands a very different quality triangle. (This is a misnomer, of course, for "quality"—being one of the newly lost absolutes—now has no more than ironic meaning.) Consider freedom. Freedom has become for us not merely an ultimate end but postmodernity's highest "spiritual" value. And justice: justice has been elevated from marvelous intermediate end, on the order of health, to something quite different from, and superior to, mere truth. Silence becomes suspect as noise is transformed into virtue. Servitude harldly has any save pejorative connotations. Inwardness, now but a memory, may soon be enemy. As to goodness and beauty: what meaning have they when everything is equally good and beautiful? And excellence, the only certain human path to beauty (and, perhaps, from beauty on to Other)—wherefore excellence when my scribbled sketches are equal to Manet's, my simpleton's equations as valid as Feynman's?

We are, in other, words witnessing the early stages of a new Western worldview. *Weltanschaaung*-shifts reveal themselves first in changed values and attitudes, then in behavior. I believe these kinds of evidence already suggest that the consequences of this change are likely to be significant and, if we are not careful, unpleasant. To cite one example, American public education, preoccupied with achieving another modern value, social progress, which is tied to freedom and justice, has for some time seemed unconcerned with demanding the development of excellence as a means of accessing truth and thus the ultimate ends like happiness. Instead, it has aspired to the secure, shared mediocrity of functional literacy. Along these lines, George Steiner has replied,

> The treason of the cleric consists of the defense of mediocrity, be it in the name of social progress; it consists of flinching from the imperative of logic, of clear thought, whatever the social perplexities to which these may lead. (1990)

I intuit that in our zeal for freedom and justice we have as a people been guilty of what Steiner calls the "cleric's treason." Are my intimations correct or wrong? I wish to know. Moreover, my students must seek their own intuitions of their culture—must ask, What is it to be human in this place and time?—and they need to develop their own inclination and power to reflect on their hunches.

Thus our interest in the realm of what I term "PopMyths," into which I propose to lead you shortly. Progress in any direction, however, requires knowledge of just where one is in the first place. Therefore, let's pause to gather our bearings by briefly considering some simple but useful truisms about culture, beliefs, behaviors and values.

## "Us" Americans: What Do We Believe? Who Are We?

For any cultural region new to one's studies—and, even more, for one's own cultural region—it is important to develop a sense of the worldviews which prevail among the inhabitants of that region. By worldview I refer to the way most people perceive their role and place within the schemata of life, especially the perceived purpose of life or at least its meaning in terms of those essential, highest qualities, the values for which people live and, if necessary, die. Cultural world- and self-views are actually much richer and deeper than that, and depend considerably on a culture's psychological, sociological and even spiritual attitudes. It is, for example, a truism that Westerners generally and Americans specifically, tend to be quite individualistic in orientation. While many of us have strong communal attachments, most Americans have (at least until recently) sought individual, not group, identity and fulfillment. A basically individualistic mindset is an important part of a so-called *modern* worldview. Members of *traditional* cultures such as the Native American, on the other hand, often tend to seek harmony and enlightenment, not separately, but as part of a larger whole or organism (e.g., the tribe or "nation"), as a drop of water returns to the ocean.

Obviously, knowing the basic nature of a culture's outlook is essential if one is to deal successfully with its members. Japan, for instance, is a country run mainly by consensus. Social harmony is assumed to be vital. Therefore, if outsiders seek to influence Japanese thought and positions on any issue they must do so before the Japanese collectively make up their mind—reach a consensus position—because after that it will be extremely difficult to do so. Americans, on the other hand, almost never reach such a consensus except during crises. Social harmony has for us seemed more a luxury than a necessity. From beginning to end on any question, sizeable numbers of citizens hold views at various points along the spectrum of opinion. Moreover, just as Americans often shift from place to place across physical landscapes, they shift about attitudinally on "mental maps" just as restlessly, changing their minds on even important issues. (For example, consider how dramatically domestic opinions have changed in the past few years regarding the importance of environmental quality, or the vitality of the American economy, or the threat of Communism.) As a consequence, Japanese car manufacturers were surprised to find it necessary to introduce all sorts of lines—luxury, moderate and inexpensive—in order to satisfy varied and changeable American tastes. They adjusted quickly.

There are many other dimensions of cultural worldviews. Cultures which have enjoyed long periods of relative socioeconomic and sociopolitical "success" (e.g., in war or economic competition) may develop an exaggerated sense of self-importance, a feeling that God is on their side, may become isolationist, xenophobic or even chauvinistic. (Some of these characteristics would probably apply about equally, during slightly offset periods, to both Japan and the United States.) Very secure cultures/nations are notable among other things for an ability to laugh at themselves, to tolerate (even encourage) difference, and to listen. Surely such peoples deserve to be described as genuinely civilized, assuming that they do in fact exist.

Conversely, a nation or culture which has repeatedly suffered great setbacks on the battlefield or in the marketplace may sometimes acquire a somewhat paranoid, chip-on-the-shoulder attitude which includes elements of both inferiority and aggression. Some nations/groups are particularly dangerous because they perceive themselves as isolated, unloved, and so perhaps are particularly likely to lash out irrationally. Israel, the Afrikkaners of South Africa, the PLO, and Iran have in recent years seemed to my mind suitable candidates.

Of course, many other important ingredients go into the complex formula of national—or regional—cultural outlook. One of the more interesting and significant of these is the sense of time. For all of us, as Samuel Johnson put it, the present passes so quickly that we can hardly think at all except in terms of the past or the future (Storr 1988). Still, perceptions of time vary dramatically according to era and place. In traditional cultures the dominant sense of time tends to be *cyclical*, that is, to emphasize the ongoing, season-like constant inconstancy of life and nature. This attitude often makes for a harmonious, empathetic acceptance of one's relationship to larger, unfolding patterns, but also—sometimes—for a degree of passivity, even fatalism. In modern societies, by contrast, the sense of time has characteristically been more *linear*; hence such expressions as "it's now or never" and "only one time around." Our Western perception that life and existence are but short interludes between incomprehensible infinities of nothingness surely explains a good deal of the frenzied nature of both our achievement and our neuroses.

It is extremely important to recognize early on that no culture's or nation's worldview is totally, or perhaps even mostly, rational or logical. Cultures and nations are assemblages of individual humans, who are firstly and lastly *emotional* beings. Logic or rationality, in other words, is built on a foundation of feelings, not the other way around. This makes analyses of cultural outlooks much more challenging than any simplistic balance sheet whereupon one totes up the debits and credits of a nation's geography, demography, ideology, economy and history. For example, you might presume that the Japanese—being today by various measures the most economically successful nation on earth—would see themselves rather as Americans did circa 1960: powerful, rich, and open to the outside world. Nothing could be further from the truth. Many Japanese still very strongly intuit themselves as poor, or at least are keenly aware of their still-recent poverty; as victims subject to the whims of an often-capricious, generally blundering superpower; and as an industrious, superior and distinctive people who should largely keep themselves separate, especially with respect to the vulgar, lazy, and badly educated parts of the rest of the world (e.g., guess who?).

How, then, does one go about figuring out what "makes a people tick," especially the members of a culture, region or nation which is new to one's study? Well, one should of course begin with a good atlas and geography primer. From these one acquires the rudiments of the general pattern and nature of the physical and cultural geography of the region or group in question. Remember, though, that such analyses are, by their very nature, mainly of the *rationalistic* elements of places; the elemental feelings in which cultures are rooted, being much more difficult to assess objectively and simplistically, are typically ignored.

One interesting way to get at least partly around this hindrance is to study some of the more distinctive dominant behaviors and popular myths of a culture as clues or guides to its citizens' values, those qualities or things they aspire to. Why not simply ask them? you might query. The answer to this perfectly reasonable question is that often people in their day-to-day behaviors do not especially reflect what they themselves believe to be the "true" or deepest nature of their culture. Consider, as one example, the maxim to "love thy neighbor as thyself," perhaps *the* defining ethic of Western Christendom. Is this really how postmodern American Christians behave?

Behaviors present one clear and useful set of clues to at least some of the important values held as part of a group's worldview. For example, in North America is it common to encounter upper- or middle-class citizens who have opted to give all their possessions to the poor and become wandering ascetics? For that matter, is it very common for people on vacation to go into the woods or mountains or desert to sit quietly for a few hours to commune with nature? No, I would argue, these are not typical behaviors. What do middle-class Americans do with, say, a few spare hours on the weekend? One nearly universal behavior is to drive (not ride a bike or walk) to a self-contained shopping mall to socialize and to shop, as we say, till we drop. Consumption, in other words, turns out on examination to be one of the most ubiquitous and fundamental "values" underlying postmodern American culture. Socializing, often closely related to consuming, also appears to be vital to most of us. We are truly world-calibre chit-chatters and schmoozers. Yet paradoxically, although we are in general not at all comfortable with physical solitude, we seem to be so emotionally or spiritually estranged from one another (as well as from nature and Other) that we have been described by social critics such as Mother Teresa as the "loneliest people on Earth."

It is at once both easy and difficult to study the popular behaviors of one's own home setting. Easy, because one thoroughly understands the language and the unique cultural fabric of the place. Difficult, curiously, for the same reasons; one is so enmeshed in this very warp and woof that it can be challenging, and uncomfortable, to extract oneself from it in order to play scientific observer for a little while. I often suggest to my beginning students that they try playing scientist the next time they visit a shopping mall to observe the prevailing human behaviors, dress and language, all of which of course offer terrific insights into attitudes, values and, ultimately, world- and self-views. "Imagine yourself," I suggest, "a stranger from, oh, Mars, just dropping in to confirm that these late-twentieth-century Americans are as you'd expect from your textbooks. Let's see, the books taught you that these people are mostly "Christians" who attend church very regularly, are independent and individualistic, yet you also learned that they stress traditional—as they say, "apple-pie"—values such as motherhood, respect for the elderly, and the like. What about it? Do the (mostly young) people you actually encounter in the mall appear to exemplify a life of loving others as much as themselves? No, not many selfless mystics, eh? Well, do they strike you as being free-thinking individualists? What, few Abe Lincolns and M. L. Kings? Humm, can we conclude then that they are traditionalists? For instance, are these young people deferential, or at least courteous, to their seniors? No? Who then are these "Americans"?

We can, in other words, get into the habit of observing human behaviors as clues to deeper meanings: What do people wear? How do they speak? What behaviors are "unacceptable"? And, of course, we can ask what each answer means in terms of the people's underlying assumptions about what is good and bad, proper and improper, desirable and detestable.

Myths are another rich source of information about a culture or nation. Technically, a myth is a legendary story, often with a hero and a moral, whose origins are lost in the dim mists of time (Campbell 1972). In popular usage, the word myth is often somewhat mistakenly used to mean a strictly imaginary fable, as in the "myth" of the Easter Bunny. The most powerful and instructive myths are frequently parables or allegories which stand as veiled explanations of the truth (ibid.). Such is the case with "popular" myths at least as much as with traditional ones like the search for the Holy Grail or the alchemists' dream of changing base metals into gold.

A culture's most popularly accepted assumptions, "truisms," and even anecdotal sayings—"people's myths" or what I shall henceforth call PopMyths—speak volumes about the world- and self-views of that culture. Many if not most of these are the expression of some deeper underlying "truths," apprehensions about meaning and quality which, due to their fundamentally intuitive nature, are rationally undefinable, even indefensible: "It's not whether you win or lose but how you play the game"; "If you're going to do it, do it right"; and so on. Popmyths offer almost unparalleled didactic access to the changing *Zeitgeist* of any people. (E.g., in the 1980s insider trading and steroid use were justified by the nihilistic PopMyth, "Winning isn't the main thing, it's the *only* thing.") Perhaps even more importantly, PopMyths can tell us of what German philosophers call a nation's "Erwartungshorizonten," its "horizons of expectation." These are the

> beliefs which shape. . .historical foresight [and] mark limits to the field of action in which. . .we see it possible to change human affairs, and so to decide which of our most cherished practical goals can be realized in fact. (Toulmin 1990)

Popmyths, in other words, offer a useful perspective on an American society which, as Ted Koppel puts it, seems largely to lack "a sense of context":

> Consider this paradox: Almost everything said publicly these days is recorded. Almost nothing of what is said is worth remembering. And what *do* we remember? Thoughts that were expressed hundreds or even thousands of years ago by philosophers, thinkers, and prophets whose ideas and principles were so universal that they endured without videotape or film. There is no culture in the world that is so obsessed as ours with immediacy. We have become so obsessed with facts that we have lost all touch with truth. (1986)

The particular PopMyths which I find to be most revealing are of three general types: those which seem passé or just plain wrong (these are rare); those which are now less appropriate than previously (less rare); and—these are the most useful, I think, as well as the most common—those which began as subtle and powerful insights but which have been so simplified or trivialized as to be virtually unrecognizable mutations of earlier truisms. I collect these, ponder them, and—after considerable rumination—try to interpret what they say about who we are. I encourage my students to do so as well, and we "compare"—i.e., argue about—our conclusions. Because this is a subjective, intuitive, almost artistic process, definitive answers are rare. The exercise can have a transformational quality to it, however, because it offers a perspective on postmodern life which many students haven't previously considered.

Postmodern American college students have grown up in a time and place dominated by a medium, television, whose only conviction has been described as "the abandonment of all conviction, the rejection of selfhood" (M. C. Miller 1985). The anthem of the postmodern age has been characterized by Milan Kundera as the sentimental, non-aesthetic aesthetic of *kitsch*, where "the dictatorship of the heart reigns supreme" (Kundera 1984). There is, Max Picard claims, no longer a world unity of the spirit or of religion or of politics, only a world unity of noise: "In it all men and all things are connected one with another" (1952). Authority in any form is anathema. Where once only the sensitive soul of the artist or saint felt *Weltschmerz* or "world pain" (Myers 1975), now we can all share Homer Simpson's sentimental pessimism.

The student's object, and that of her teacher, is the recognition and the pursuit of the genuine. This is not to suggest that there is no place for the sentimental inauthenticity of kitsch. Most of us enjoy the easy mediocrity of fast—faux—food or the false tears of a pulp novel or a soap opera from time to time. Besides, occasional contact with the counterfeit, the simulation, may in fact be necessary if the authentic is to be truly appreciated. (I am confident, for instance, that one's appreciation of such human singularities as Mother Teresa or Vaclav Havel increases with experience of the world-as-it-is.) However, kitsch pursued out of ignorance is quite something else; for only alienation, angst and anomie—the triad which together appear to be a postmodern leitmotif—can lie at the end of a path which seeks, for whatever reason, to avoid the full human experience of existence.

Mark Crispin Miller has argued that "as you watch [television], there is no Big Brother out there watching you—not because there isn't a Big Brother, but because Big Brother is you, watching" (1985). Popmyths offer the unique opportunity to turn the tables again by allowing us to watch ourselves watching.

Below I discuss a selection of representative postmodern American PopMyths circa early 1990s. Doubtless there are many other telling American "people's myths"; these are no more than personal favorites. My students and I find it enlightening and entertaining to ask such questions as, What did this expression mean originally? What does it mean now? Who, in other words, were we, who are we, and who are we becoming? The last of these is the key. Encouraging students to come to grips with the question Who shall I be? is the real purpose of the exercise.

Before getting on to the PopMyths themselves I should mention another point or two. Firstly, some of our newer people's myths sound terrific but on reflection turn out to be both too ambitious and too simplistic: "All you need is love"; "Don't worry, be happy"; "I feel good about feeling good about myself"; "Small is beautiful" (how many of us who fancy ourselves environmentalists have actually abandoned our cars?); even "Kids are people too" (am I mistaken in hearing a little avoidance of responsibility in that lovely phrase?); and "It's never too late to have a happy childhood." One recalls older, humbler, more ingenuous PopMyths, now as dated as mastodons, which, tugging at the heartstrings, echo from the past like the voices of unquiet spirits: "Life is just a bowl of cherries"; "There's no place like home"; and "Bigger is better" (an old favorite in Texas), for example. On examination, however, such maxims appear rather like prescriptions of aspirin for relief of a brain tumor.

Secondly, some time-honored American truisms seem to my students and me as appropriate as ever. "An apple a day keeps the doctor away"; "No pain no gain"; "The truth hurts"; and "It's too good to be true" all still ring true, we think.

And, thirdly, there are some contemporary people's myths which say a good deal about late-twentieth-century American values, among which "The winners are the ones with the most stuff when they die" and "Whoever said money can't buy happiness didn't know where to shop" have to be the saddest. Such facile cynicism seems to verify W. B. Yeats's post-World War I poetic prophecy of loss and decline: "Things fall apart; the center cannot hold."

One does, however, begin to hear what sound to be new "people's paradigms" which are characterized more than anything else by uncertainty: "Things happen"; "Things change" (the title of a recent popular American film); and even—borrowed from Yeats as noted above—"Things fall apart" (Storr 1988), for instance. The very fuzziness of these postmodern perspectives is impressive, for they seem to accurately reflect our contemporary understanding of the inconstancy and indeterminacy of existence itself. The humility of this attitude, together with a concomitant and refreshing diminution of hubris, is encouraging. The great paradox of the universe as we now understand it is that it is equally cosmic and chaotic, both regular and random. On balance, it seems to me that a society in which large numbers of people intuit that "life is a beach" *and* that "shit happens" is probably headed, however obliquely, in the right direction.

## PopMyth 1: Everyone is beautiful in his/her own way.

This is a lovely and poetic statement of a fundamental truth about the unique nature of each frail but wondering human creature. However, in our interpretation of it—or, perhaps, in our *application* of it—a peculiarly American strain of wishful thinking creeps in, that is, the thought that *all* people are beautiful *always*. Where once we reassured ourselves with the humbling, realistic truth that, after all, "nobody's perfect," now we sentimentally kid ourselves that, in effect, "everybody's perfect."

My reply to this one day, when I was in a particularly curmudgeonly mood, was, "If that's so, where did all the schmucks come from?" Humans by their very nature not only have the *potential* to be ugly, they all *are* ugly, sometimes, even our Mother Teresas, of whom the supply is sadly short. (A mutual friend in Calcutta assures me that Mother T. has been known to be pretty unsympathetic toward selfish personalities.) "Everyone is stupid" is, in other words, precisely as accurate, and as limited, a truth as "everyone is beautiful." It is a sign of our immaturity that we are uncomfortable with the darker sides of our nature.

## PopMyth 2: You are only as old as you feel.

This is one of my favorite American axioms. One has only to examine people to verify that it works: believers in this myth live more fulfilled, probably even longer lives than skeptics. In part, it expresses the fact that humans, being especially "aware" and "wondering" and "problem-solving" entities, may in important ways actually improve as their physical bodies age and decay, at least while mental faculties are unimpaired. More importantly, it seems to get at the deep truth that life is not a spectator sport. It must be engaged fully, moment by moment, or it is wasted.

Americans, perhaps in part because of our aging population, now seem determined to kill a wonderful metaphor by transforming it into literal truth. You perhaps read the recent news story which reported that a sizeable majority of Americans defined "middle age" as the years 46 to 75. And twenty-nine percent of the respondents insisted that middle age even extends *beyond* 75! Is this not simply self-deception? Even today, most men die before age 90 and most women prior to 95. Does not this fanaticism about "youth" and "middle age" say that in some worrisome way we have lost our respect for, and our ability to reconcile ourselves to, our own mortality?

## PopMyth 3: Every student can learn.

Yes. As much as any other, this maxim represents the central touchstone of American life. Our entire culture is built on the hope of liberating our citizens through universal and free education. (If for nothing else, history will recall us fondly for the sheer audacity of our hopefulness.) In significant ways, "Every student can learn" is a variation on "Everyone is beautiful" in that the object of life is to live as radiantly, as "beautifully" if you will, as possible given the unavoidable external limits beyond one's control. Larry Bird and Magic Johnson may not have been the pure athletes that Michael Jordan is, for example, but consider what they did with the gifts they had. Every student has potential. The aim of formal education is the maximum realization of that potential.

How can he possibly complain about this one? you may ask. I have no argument with the philosophical underpinnings of this myth, which seem to me to be very close to the same as those of "Every person has equal worth in the eyes of God." My concern is, again, with the manner in which we interpret or apply this principle, and what this implies about how we see ourselves. Two points are worth noting. First, achieving one's potential is never easy. Just the opposite, it is *always* difficult. Riding an elevator to the top of the Empire State Building is not the same as climbing Everest. The scriptures do not inform us that the road to heaven is easy and the gate wide. Rather, they inform us that "it is easier for a camel to pass through the eye of a needle than for a rich person to enter paradise"; that the road to happiness is to "give your possessions to the poor and follow the higher path"; and so on. Any fool knows that the race doesn't go to the couch potato. If self-esteem is the key to personal happiness, self-discipline is the key to personal accomplishment.

Second, there *are* limits which apply to all of us. However, some of them vary in degree from person to person. We are all equally mortal, but Einstein was far smarter than I am and David Robinson is far more athletic than I can ever hope to be. Should I be ashamed of my limits? I think not.

What I think "Every student can learn" means is that each student can pursue her or his maximum potential given hard work, commitment, and the good fortune of nuturing, caring, and supportive familial, societal and education systems. I fear that for us, today, that formula seems excessively tough, and this bothers me for, as a scientist, I can never completely forget that there are limits. Nature has teeth, after all. Those who lose sight of the fact that life is fundamentally a struggle (albeit the most wonderful of struggles) will be quite unselfconsciously shouldered into history's dustbin of memorabilia by those who do not, in much the same way as the success of market economies has rendered state socialism almost embarrassingly redundant.

## PopMyth 4: "Have a nice day."

This quintessentially American phrase reveals us at our best and, perhaps, at just about our worst. One recalls the possibly apocryphal story of the curmudgeonly Briton who responded to this injunction with, "No, thanks. I have other plans." Sometimes when check-out clerks tell me to "have a nice day," I can tell that they really mean it. They mean to wish me well, perhaps even to recognize a spark of the Divine in me, as Hindus do when they greet one with a smile, a nod, and a pressing together of the palms. This is terrific stuff. But sometimes "Have a nice day" merely represents a barely civil version of "Whoever you were, you're outa here now." This isn't all bad: we like the security, and civility, of pat phrases which say "hi" and "bye" with at least the illusion of more than the passing interest. Still, we diminish important words through repeatedly careless usage. Ask yourself, for instance, whether such once-potent words as "love" or "God" or—especially—"nice" carry the weight they once had.

A larger concern that the ubiquity of "Have a nice day" raises is the fear that it smacks of an American tendency to trivialize desires. A "nice" day always makes me think of finding someone else's package of Twinkies in my grocery sack. Images of speaking to the U.N. General Assembly or learning sky-diving definitely do not come to mind. Shouldn't we be wishing one another challenging days, or tranquil days, or even terrible days? Can I seriously envision George Washington, Black Elk or Martin Luther King, Jr., encouraging me to "have a nice day"?

On the other hand, they might surprise me. If civilization rests more on modest civility than on sincerity, as geographer-philosopher Yi-Fu Tuan argues, "H.A.N.D." could qualify on either count.

## PopMyth 5: All things are possible.

This myth works beautifully as an often self-fulfilling prophecy as long as we don't take it literally. It expresses our abiding *hopefulness* about our ability, and our willingness, to transcend apparent or assumed limits. Call it the Spud Webb syndrome: a committed little guy can occasionally outdunk the big guys but more importantly can always "grow" by the effort. This is *not* a simple-minded optimism which believes that things are bound to get better. Still, it does suggest that something in us deeply resents the fact that nature cannot be fooled. Where did we get such presumption?

**PopMyth 6:  I *love* (pizza) (the Bulls) (silk sheets) (a cold beer) (my Porsche) (whatever)!**

No, you don't.  You may "love" yourself, your family, maybe even some other humans, aspects of nature, and God, but you cannot "love" Disney World, money, or even the World Series.  Such leveling of the language inevitably diminishes the meaning of a phrase like "I love you," not to mention "God is love" (compare PopMyth 4).  Far worse is the implication that we have allowed ourselves to become alienated from things of real worth.  A croupy toddler squalling in the middle of the night has an intrinsic beauty or quality which a pepperoni pizza can never have, "bottom lines" notwithstanding.

**PopMyth 7:  You gotta go for the gusto because you only get one shot at the brass ring and it's now or never (etc.).**

In the Western world, we largely perceive our lives, and time itself, as linear, proceeding from a distinct beginning to a clear ending.  People in traditional societies tend to fit individual lives into a more cyclical sense of time, as part of the gradual unfolding of an ongoing process.  The "arrow of time" metaphor has served Americans remarkably well, for it led—almost pointed—to all sorts of wonderful advances, from air conditioning and *Huck Finn* on audiotape to same-day delivery of the *New York Times* in the middle of nowhere.

Every quality has its shadow, however.  Consider how perverted seems our American Halloween—whose anthem was captured by Charles Schultz's Sally: "I only want my fair share!"—compared with the celebration of the Day of the Dead (All Souls Day) in Mexico, a time when people gather at cemeteries to celebrate and to remember.  Here is a clear case where we have carried a good thing too far.  Our fanatical lust to get "our fair share" while we can threatens the very integrity of the planetary ecosystem, being unconcerned with a "fair share" for future generations.  We crave youthfulness because we resent the cosmic insult of mortality.  We even abhor the "daily death" of work—how many American lottery-winners reveal plans to pursue community service or meaningful work?—because it uses up precious time we could be "spending" shopping or watching TV.

**PopMyth 8:  Just say no.**

The simple power of "Just say no" lies in the recognition that we *can* take control of ourselves and that, finally, we are responsible for ourselves.

"Empowerment" and mastery are to be found only at the end of this road, and as the Chinese say, a journey of a thousand miles begins with one step. However, to imply that after the first step the rest of the thousand miles is a foregone conclusion or that taking the first step obviates the need to continue the journey exaggerates the importance of intention. *All* the worthwhile roads in life are uphill, take (usually heroic) effort, and require some help along the way.

### PopMyth 9:  We're Number One!

Any comment would be superfluous, except to recall that a generation or so ago we *didn't* say this because we *were*, and now that we *aren't*, we *do*. Sigh.

### PopMyth 10:  If it doesn't work, throw it out.

Octavio Paz, the celebrated Mexican intellectual, used to write admiringly of American expediency.  He meant that unlike the institutions of many traditonal societies, those of America were not "sacred" but existed solely to function.  Moreover, when our institutions have stopped working, we've usually opted for new ones or at least new forms of old ones. (Consider, for example, that the vast majority of Americans consider themselves capitalists *and* approve of an old-age social security system; or that baseball is no longer everyone's idea of the national pastime; or how little apple pie is actually consumed nowadays; or even the way motherhood is viewed as the century winds down.)

It is worth noting, however, that our American expediency seems always to have rested historically on a collective vision of the worth and meaning of the individual person, *and* on the idea of service to God (or to some transcendence), and therefore on a concern for a shared common good. As a national ethic expediency seems recently to have devolved, for we have become a society whose core values encourage a discarding of tangible history and a depletion of resources in the name of a very different kind of expediency.

### PopMyth 11:  If it walks like a duck, quacks like a duck and looks like a duck, it's a duck.

This notion reflects, I think, our abiding faith in *rational* knowledge or "mind over matter" (see Chapter VII).  This approach has taken us a long way, indeed: wonders like polio vaccines, microwave ovens and mountain bikes came from our belief that the universe is understandable and our dogged pursuit of measurable and verifiable evidence. However, some very important understandings—including arguably *all* of the highest, such as beauty or quality, or the intrinsic superiority of love to hate, life to death, truth to untruth, or knowledge to ignorance—do not appear to be fundamentally rational or logical but are rooted in other kinds of knowledge, intuitive or revelatory or what-have-you (see Chapter II). As another popular American myth reminds us, appearances can be deceiving. Donald Duck walks, quacks and looks (sort of) like a duck, but is less like a real duck than I am. A simple-minded suspension of critical judgment does not serve us well. Consider how many political leaders we've elected in recent decades who looked, walked and talked like statesmen, but whose appearance turned out to be as much a caricature as Walt Disney's.

## PopMyth 12: Beauty is only skin deep.

Of course, what this actually means is, the appearance of beauty is only skin deep but *real* beauty—beauty of heart, mind and soul—is deep, lasting and finer than any quality save love. Thus anyone could observe the luminous beauty of a Mother Teresa or a Gandhi, neither of whom would be likely to register a "10" on Donald Trump's or Madonna's scale of looks.

Whether or not we as a people still believe that beauty is only skin deep is an open question. If so, why are so many of us wearing braces at 40 or 50 or even 60 years of age? More important is the question of whether we still believe in "beauty" at all: if everyone is equally beautiful all the time, is anyone really beautiful? (See PopMyth Number 1.)

## PopMyth 13: It's the thought that counts.

Unconditional love is what this myth is all about. It says, "It's okay that you forgot to take the pizza out of the oven again, you schmuck." Perfection is not attainable, probably not even desirable, but genuineness is.

There is a limit to the worth of good intentions, however, one which we increasingly ignore to avoid being judgmental. Alas, the universe cannot be fooled, as physicist Richard Feynman put it, and we try to deceive it at our own peril. All the meant-tos on earth count for naught if I crash my motorcycle without my helmet. As Frederick Buechner put it, "When Jesus talked to the Pharisees, he didn't say, 'There, there. Everything's going to be all right.' He said, 'You brood of vipers! how can you speak good when you are evil!' And he said that to them because he loved them" (1973).

## PopMyth 14:  The object of life is the pursuit of happiness.

Only a fool would attack this Americanism.  "Life, liberty and the pursuit of happiness":  it's right there in the Declaration of Independence, isn't it, just as it has been from the beginning?  Well, yes and no.  All of us still desire happiness, which most of us still associate with such "ultimate ends" as harmony, fulfillment, understanding, identity and tranquility.  However, it is significant that Jefferson did not borrow John Locke's quotation verbatim, which was "life, liberty and the pursuit of *property*."  It does appear that many of us have begun to confuse *pleasure*—which can be "pursued" directly, by purchasing an ice-cream cone, for instance—with *happiness*, which, like love, can only be found unselfconsciously and through service to something besides one's self.  Otherwise, as Calvin (of "Calvin and Hobbes" comic-strip fame) put it recently, "When you're *serious* about having fun, it's not much fun at all!"

## PopMyth 15:  God is love.

Only a very great fool would question this one.  So, here goes.  The big mystery about existence, as anyone over 40 knows, is existence itself.  Why are we?  Why is anything?  Is the universe merely accidental?  What's it all about, Alfie?  "Love" is an answer which appeals to many of us in a profound if inexpressible way.  Likewise, however incomprehensible the nature of the ultimate may be, we intuit that it must somehow be like those qualities we call beauty, goodness and love, or even that these are our inadequate conceptions of that which some call God.  No one—however agnostic—who has once fully glimpsed the dazzling beauty of a sunrise, a crying baby or a daffodil can deny the glorious, otherworldly sensation that Edward Abbey called the "shock of the real."

(He's playing at Romantic Poet again, you say?  I think not, really, but you be the judge: a romantic is one who longs not to understand and identify with things as they are but wishes to—abracadabra!—conjure an entirely different, preferred order.  At bottom, one's cosmology can be either magical or awe-full.  All others are just permutations of one or the other.)

Still, God is surely not merely "love" in any strictly saccharine, cutesy-wootsey, sentimental sense.  As real as is nature's *beauty* is its sheer power or, in Joseph Campbell's words, its *horror*.  We only have to stare into the pitiless eyes of a great carnivore, or wade into a pounding surf, or stand amidst a torrential gale, to experience both of these mysterious qualities.  What do we make of them?  From the perspective of Hindus (and some Christian mystics), not only is the difference between "good" and "evil" an illusion created by us—e.g., the colony of pill bugs in my tomato patch may seem evil to me but is the best of possible worlds to the bugs themselves—but the sublime beauty and the awful power equally reflect the always-so. (In fact, faith seems to me as much as anything the willing acceptance of what seems a fundamentally contradictory duality.) In other words, while many of us may feel compelled to choose sides in a moral argument and reject such monistic viewpoints, perhaps we should hesitate to presume to judge that which we cannot comprehend. Asked to describe God, Hindus answer: "Neti, neti," not this, not that. "To say that love is God is romantic idealism. To say that God is love is either the last straw or the ultimate truth" (Buechner 1973).

I cannot leave this PopMyth without remarking on the fact that "God is dead" has become about as literal or trite and therefore as dead a metaphor as has "God is love." Recall that the central theme of this book is, one might say, about staying centered in a time when, because the very idea of centeredness appears to have been slain, such an ambition smacks, at best, of archaic naiveté. A Taoist-postmodernist (e.g., like me) finds an almost paleontological exposing of successive unsatisfactory certainties quite delightful, for they seem steps which lead ever deeper down toward Truth or call-it-what-you will. Put another way, the *real* reason why this kind of process reveals the typically sardonic sense of humor of the always-so is that it sounds a warning to those seekers-after-understanding who would listen. It goes something like, "Beware! Turn back. This way lies nonstop return to Go via Hubris, which ain't no Love Boat!" We are in other words reassured that uncertainty's present certainty is, if you will pardon the expression, virtually certain to be another mask of the always-so. What a kidder.

## PopMyth 16: It's not whether you win or lose, it's how you play the game *versus* Winning isn't the main thing, it's the only thing.

These two sports metaphors remind us of some fundamental changes in the American collective psyche over the past generation or two, particularly the importance in our society of fair play—to use an expression so dated it sounds archaic—relative to success. I grew up in the middle of the middle class, in the middle part of this century and in the middle part of the United States. Back in 1950, my contemporaries and I must have been instructed that "it's how you play the game!" on at least a weekly basis, but even then we suspected there was more to the game than that. (Like most kids we were ignorant, not stupid.) Although we did not know that Americans could afford the luxury of fair play partly because our wealth was built on cheap materials and lots of grinding labor in other parts of the world, we knew darned well that sometimes *results do count*. If a schoolyard bully commandeered our favorite comic book or catcher's mask, that was a real and significant loss, all the principles in the world notwithstanding.

Consider by contrast the equivalent American sports metaphor of these closing decades of the twentieth century: "Winning isn't the main thing, it's the *only* thing!" Although this myth was popularized by Green Bay Packer coach Vince Lombardi, his use of the image was clearly metaphorical, not literal: for instance, no one who knew Lombardi could conceive of him bribing a referee in order to win a game. *How* he won was very important to him. Somehow over the past generation we have begun to take this expression at its face value. "Maybe winning—that is, success—*is* the only thing," we think, buffeted as we are by the pressures and outrages of an uncaring world. "If it takes steroids or insider trading to win, so be it."

More even than on education, democracy is built on shared *trust*. Alexis de Tocqueville intimated that if a democratic society becomes "selfish"—i.e., operates on a basis of each individual aiming for maximum short-term personal benefit rather than out of a self-interest rooted in the common good—that nation is in trouble. It is one thing to have a nation of Lombardi-style warriors, who *say* that "winning is the only thing" but whose actual play reflects the knowledge that a dishonorable victory is worthless; but a nation of Ivan Boeskys and Marion Barrys, for whom success *is* both means and end, is very different and very disturbing, for that way lies not only unhappiness but, perversely enough, failure.

## PopMyth 17: Equity is more important than quality and/or my opinion is as good as yours.

It is worth repeating: nothing is more important in a democracy than a perception of fair play, the trust that everybody is equal in the eyes of the law. Although in an ideal world we would prefer an electorate composed exclusively of well-educated and contemplative voters, in the real world nations governed by everyone are superior to those run by an elite few. (If you doubt this, ask yourself which future is worse, one in which poorly educated, disadvantaged inner-city residents *participate* in the political process or one in which they do not.)

On the other hand, every *person* is assumed to be of equal worth, not every *idea*. Trust in fair play, as we have said, has been perceived in our national culture to be even more fundamental than personal ownership of a car, a home or a TV. Although the principle of equity outweighs all others with respect to people, it cannot do so in the realm of ideas. *All ideas or principles are not equal.* This is transparently clear to 99% of us, yet somehow we are no longer comfortable acknowledging its truth. Because it offends our egalitarian sensibilities for a seven-footer to be favored in basketball, we not only root for the Spud Webbs of the world but try to convince ourselves that, hey, size doesn't make any difference in basketball, does it? It's pretty to think so, but the hard truth is that the average height of NBA players is six-eight and climbing for a reason.

So it is with ideas: "superior" ones have withstood the test of careful, objective scrutiny. At one time the vast majority of people considered the earth to be the center of the solar system. Obvious, but wrong. In the eighteenth century, before the discovery of oxygen, scientists believed that an enclosed candle eventually flickered out because the flame produced too great a concentration of phlogiston. There is no such substance as phlogiston! Half the members of a talk-show audience may believe the earth to be flat or the stars to be pinpricks in a velvet ceiling but, to be blunt, so what?

This is neither elitist snobbery nor abstract, ivory-tower philosophy. Surely part of the erosion of both our public school system and our economy stems from our having forgotten that, in the context of institutions such as formal education, *quality* must be the first principle because only it *can* be the first principle. Nothing else works. All you have to do to convince yourself this is so is to examine another American institution in which quality *is* sacrosanct: sports. Ask one hundred serious fans to name the top ten baseball or football or basketball players or golfers or hockey players and you will overwhelmingly hear the same names mentioned.

"If something is worth doing, it is worth doing well," the moralists have repeatedly warned. "There is no free lunch." These are hard maxims, so unforgiving that it is not unreasonable that we should try to escape or at least ignore them. Alas, it cannot be, and the time when we could excuse ignorance on the grounds of innocence is over.


## PopMyth 18: Work to live, don't live to work.

Sometimes this PopMyth connotes, "Remember to stop and smell the roses," doesn't it? For a people as compulsive as we, this reminder reconnects us with the deep and abiding truth that life, as the Italians say, is a verb. Sometimes, however, we take this PopMyth to mean, "Work is to be avoided." When American lottery-winning millionaires describe their plans, typically they intend to quit work and "take it easy." People who are trapped in mindless work understandably lust for the "freedom" to do nothing. These run the risk, however, of pursuing an illusion: around the world, across virtually all cultural and historical lines, human beings have found meaningful work to be one of the handful of paths—along with love, compassion and selflessness—to true happiness.

## PopMyth 19: Life is sacred.

This is one of our most persistent people's myths. Although we might interpret "sacred" in various ways, most of us believe strongly that there is something transcendently worthwhile about living things. I suspect that the even humblest dandelion would be rated in a poll as more precious or special than the best artificial bouquet ever made.

But, of course, the sanctity of life has never been all that simple an idea. Traditionally the majority of us have considered some lives to be somehow more sacred than others. Hundreds of millions of yeasts are killed each time a loaf of bread is baked, yet we are all bread-eaters. Likewise, not only are our children more worthwhile than dandelions but their lives are, for many of us, ranked ahead of our own. Even ideas can sometimes rank above life: martyrs by definition consider life less important than spiritual integrity.

Postmodern life, especially, is so difficult, complex and full of choices that this PopMyth is fuzzier than ever. How sacred are the lives of octo-genarians on expensive life-support systems in a nation with unhealthy children? How sacred were the millions fetuses aborted in the United States in the past few decades? How sacred were the many who have suffered and starved while we have enjoyed luxuries beyond Croesus' wildest dreams? Regardless of one's ideological persuasion, these are real and troubling questions which are likely to become even more difficult.


## PopMyth 20: Great!

Whatever happened to "good"? This is not merely a matter of the leveling and diminishment of the language, which is troubling enough (see PopMyths 4 and 6). If McDonald's french fries are "great," what then are strawberries and cream in one's honeymoon suite? Why everything this side of "it sucks" must be "great" is the question which bothers me. "Great" just possibly may be our most ubiquitous Freudian slip, a reminder of the extent to which we pursue those qualities we associate with greatness—power (or control) and notoriety—rather than those of goodness. The figures who appear on the lists of heroes of adolescent Americans are nearly all distinguished by, and known for, their wealth, power and fame. By this standard a "great" Napoleon surmounts a merely "good" George Washington. It has long been a huckster's axiom that sizzle is easier to create and to sell than steak. Fair enough, but however you hype it, "sizzle" turns out to be insubstantial fare.

## PopMyth 21:  Shit happens, BUT Life is a beach.

I know, I know: like "Don't worry, be happy," these sound like so much cheap, simple-minded psychdrivel. They can be and often are. In the face of a tragedy, say, a child with AIDS, or even a major setback, like being fired, the hollow comfort of either "Life is a beach!" or "Shit happens" would be nothing short of insulting. And I concede that the latter sometimes is a kind of witlessly aggressive ersatz Taoism, e.g., "I nearly caused an accident on the freeway? Hey, dude, shit happens!" Still, I find the combination of these two myths, especially among the young, encouraging. We are a people for whom the dark side of life has traditionally posed great difficulty: pain, suffering death and, maybe most of all, failure. Unlike Thomas Edison, who considered his first five thousand light-bulb designs to be successes (in that he learned that they didn't work), for most of us failure seems somehow bad, un-American; and it is dangerous to presume, as we once did, that things are constantly getting better and better if they are not, as the present environmental and economic crises make abundantly clear. But a generation which has learned to persevere because and in spite of unpleasant stuff happening, still seeking a "beach" of a life, has perhaps managed to avoid being waylaid by cynicism by exchanging that earlier, aggressively optimistic American innocence (which no longer seems very appropriate) for a hopeful realism. We are growing up. I am beginning to believe that one not-too-distant day the world will wake up to an America which can pass that ultimate test of civilization, the ability to laugh at its own shortcomings.

### Note

1. Art and music offer even straighter avenues, although the very directness of these paths renders them treacherous, for they lead as often to illusions and nightmares as to realities. Still, ten minutes invested in any Midwestern talk radio show, along with fifteen minutes of rock videos on MTV, twenty minutes of *Dances With Wolves* (the *Red River* or *Gone With the Wind* of its day) and a full half-hour episode of "The Simpsons" offer a cornucopia of revelations concerning postmodern America, one far more bounteous than, say, a semester reading social and political theory or literary criticism at Berkeley. This is so because Bart Simpson and Ice T. don't merely speak about *Zeitgeist* but—like Neil Armstrong and the cathedral builders at Chartres—*are* metaphors for the spirit of their times. Undoubtedly these natural sons of *fin-de-siècle* American *Weltanschauung* are by virtue of their authenticity nearer primary sources than are mere scholastic abstractions like Economic and Political Man. Still, it is important to remember that even the most genuine pop culture images are finally limited, secondary effects far more than they are causes.

## Review and Reflections on the Text

1.      Define *Zeitgeist*; the "Other"; antinomy; PopMyth; *Erwartungs-horizonten*; *Welschmertz*; angst.

2.      Consider the proposition that "There are . . . only socially created realities" and Lewis Thomas's response that he believes "only a little of this." Which part(s) of the proposition do you suppose Thomas believes? Which do you believe?

3.      Try constructing a "quality triangle" that represents the way you rank goals and ideals in your own life and the ways they support or depend on each other. To do this, you will need to ponder some of the following questions (and probably others as well): Is freedom an ultimate end in itself? Is justice related to truth? Is it superior or inferior to truth? What do servitude, inwardness, harmony, fulfillment, beauty, and excellence mean to you? How would you explain the reasons for your answers?

4.      In what sense is functional literacy a goal that compromises the drive toward excellence? How has social progress been used in the "defense of mediocrity" as George Steiner implies?

5.      The author notes that "Americans . . . almost never reach . . . a consensus except during crises." How is *consensus* different from majority rule? Can you recall crises when American culture has been galvanized into consensus? What are the benefits of consensus? What are the dangers?

6.      The author draws connections between the relative "success" of nations/cultures and their characteristic worldviews. Do you see similar connections between the experience of *individuals* and *their* worldviews? Explain your answer and reflect on the implications.

7.      Explain the difference between cyclical and linear concepts of time. How does each affect perceptions of the present?

8.      Why are behaviors and popular myths useful in identifying cultural values? Why are they more "troublesome" than the raw data found in atlases and textbooks? Why do behaviors sometimes appear to contradict popular myths?

9.      Try pretending you are an extraterrestrial on a fact-gathering field trip to the United States. What kinds of places (other than a shopping mall)

would be likely sites for observing typical behaviors? What might you gather about American cultural values from observing election politics? From comparing the popularity of various forms of leisure activity and amusements? From comparing attitudes toward various professions? From reading *The Wall Street Journal* or *The National Enquirer* or another daily newspaper? From watching your local nightly television news broadcast? A national network news broadcast? From listening to programming on various radio stations (top-40, oldies, public radio, country/western, news/talk, evangelical, classical, and jazz)?

10.     List some forms of kitsch you encounter or have encountered. In what sense is the pursuit of kitsch also the avoidance of full, genuine experience? Explain your answer in terms of your own encounters with kitsch.

11.     Choose a few of the twenty-one PopMyths the author discusses and write a paragraph or two in which you explore your own reflections on their original and current meanings.

12.     Form a group with several other students and together come up with two PopMyths the author has not identified. Each of you might reflect separately on these PopMyths in writing and then compare and discuss your reflections.

# V. Beyond Kitsch*

> The true exercise of freedom is—cannily and wisely and with grace—to move inside what space confines.
>
> —A. S. Byatt, *Possession*

Good morning. To steal one of Ken Boulding's lines, it is always a pleasure for a decaying old mind to grind some favorite axes before some trapped, decaying *young* minds. In my own classes I would as soon tout astrology as express my personal political or religious opinions, but *here*, well, who among you could allow such helpless victims as yourselves to escape unenlightened?

Not long ago, a friend complained that I was "the worst possible combination of conservative and liberal: you believe," she charged, "that people are individually responsible for themselves and their problems, but that the only solution to these problems lies in collective action rooted in a sense of connectedness. I never know if I'm talking to Margaret Thatcher or Jesse Jackson." Quite so. While I have nothing against ideologies per se, I do deeply mistrust dogmatists, for the surest lesson of postmodern science is the irreducible fuzziness of Nature. In other words, the assumption of certainty is virtually always an exercise in self-deception.

A popular Christmas carol informs us that "He rules the world with Truth and Grace." How innocuous the literal words, how weighty the meaning. (Who can forget Thomas Jefferson's fear, contemplating slavery, that God may have intended it when he promised to be "just"?) As Joseph Campbell liked to point out, the two fundamental attributes evident in all of existence are absolute beauty (or quality, if you prefer) and sublime—horrible—power. Both come under the heading of Truth, do they not?

---

*A guest lecture delivered November 26, 1990, to a senior-level class in the politics of China.

61

As to Grace, a Confucian would argue that it is *not* one of the direct, natural aspects of the cosmic warp and woof like beauty and horror but *is* a quality which comes into being only through the unfettered action of sentient mortals like you and me. Grace in this sense may well be our main purpose. Or potentiality, if you like. (When can one be truly certain one is speaking only metaphorically? Every student of Asian thought-systems is haunted by the suspicion [Goethe's, I think, or Joyce's] that *everything* is a metaphor. . .) Furthermore, the Confucian believes that the grace of compassion is accessible only to the person who can stand, clear-eyed, to tilt with the Exquisite and the Awful on the plains of Truth. Like a rose, the universe has teeth. If you doubt this, go to Padre Island the next time a hurricane is approaching from the Gulf of Mexico. Stand in the pounding surf—if you can. Feel the mindless, heartless gale blow over you, through you. Gaze into the void that is the bottomless, pathless sky. It's all gorgeous, yes, but also monstrous.

It is possible that evil exists because of our failings ("sin" or "attachment," for instance), but the sheer "badness" or horror of death, decay, entropy, suffering, things eating other things—we have nothing to do with this. It's simply written into the script. You and I might have written a kinder, gentler screenplay, but we weren't consulted. One of the commonalities of most Oriental philosophical systems is the assumption that unless and until you can accept the Truth as it is—both beautiful and horrible—you are stuck at the level of illusion and thus, so far as the manifestation of grace is concerned, impotent. Is not 'faith' in fact an acceptance of—better, a willing submission to—the apparently irreducible duality of these qualities, the beauty and the horror? And besides, as Richard Feynman put it, we try to kid Nature at our own peril. But yes, I do think that we are autonomous and responsible for ourselves.

May I relate a small personal story? (It is not my nature to reveal my frayed edges to my students, but my darned philosophy students this term have, as Antoine de Saint-Exupéry puts it, "tamed" me. Most disconcerting.) One day, around 1930, when my father was twelve or thirteen, he awoke to discover that his father had abandoned the family—my grandmother, my aunt, and Dad—forever. From that day on, my dad worked at least part-time, and never got beyond high school. One day at roughly the same time, when my mother was about fourteen, she discovered her father—an unemployed coal miner, a relatively young man—dead in the back yard. This was during the Depression: no safety net of welfare or Social Security buffered the family from hunger and despair. They were on their own. Mom's elder sister dropped out of college to support the six children, and my mother, like my father, never attended university.

Is the point of my little story that I've come from an exceptionally harsh background? Quite the contrary. Given a few variations, mine is the human story. To live is to suffer. Scratch even a rich, powerful or beautiful person deeply enough and you'll reach the smell of pain, decay and death, the scent of humanness.

Did these travails make my mom and dad a little crazy? you ask. Sure. But they persevered. This is not a rehearsal, ladies and gentleman. Alas, there *is* no rehearsal for life. You have to make it up as you go along, and just when you are getting your lines down, off the stage you go. If it seems unfair, even if it *is* unfair, so what? You've just appeared out of a void to which you must soon return. This is Mystery with a capital M. If you spend all your energy complaining of a rose's thorns, you never experience its fragrance. Enjoy and be grateful for the sheer wonder of being. In fact, genuine enjoyment is *always* derived of the wonder of gratitude and the freedom of autonomy.

So, I reiterate, like any good quasi-Neo-Confucian (more about that shortly), I *do* believe in the worth and centrality of the individual experience.

On the other hand, what's the use of any self-authority and -experience isolated from community, that is, from unity? The true intent of what we in the West call self-development lies in the ingenuous hope that through it one just might achieve the sage's level of identification with, and thus responsibility for, the Other.

You have grown up in an age in which the purpose of life is taken to be pleasure: sex, drugs and rock'n'roll; Porsches and Porterhouse steaks; season tickets and Acapulco. Whatever. Accept that if you must, but at least do so with eyes wide open. Most of the lasting philosophical systems, Eastern and Western, suggest that the deeper you settle within your own self, the more true pleasure (and pain, of course) you are sure to experience. Should your goal be *happiness*, however, that's another matter altogether. As the Christian existentialist Søren Kierkegaard put it, the more you seek satisfaction, the greater your frustration. The great moral cartographers instruct that the only avenues to happiness seem to be *external*: that is, achieved by identifying with something—ideals, ideas, or other people—which transcends your personal interests, by actions not driven by desire; and by a cleansing of the heart (Radhakrishnan and Moore 1957).

Moreover, as you've doubtless noticed, this is neither a simple nor an easy age. It is a time of fuzzy uncertainty, change, and (this is the killer) paradox rather than absolutes. (As Kenneth Boulding likes to say, even in science we have found that "all important distinctions are unclear.") Not surprisingly, angst (dread), anomie (a sense that things are out of control) and ennui (weariness, boredom or general dissatisfaction) are rampant. And, if so many of our best and brightest are alienated (check out the middle-class teenage suicide rate), what can we expect among the Bart Simpsons and Willie Hortons, the poorest, least educated and most marginal? Mother Teresa of Calcutta claims that it will be easier to cure the Third World's problems of disease and hunger than the First World's despair and "aloneness." In other words, our social ills are beyond those tidy "solutions" which might have worked only a few generations ago. Will the lost souls of the inner cities fix themselves because we moralists shout, "Cut that out! Shape up! Be responsible!"? I think not.

Let me offer an example of how complicated and interconnected is the flawed weave of the postmodern social fabric by contrast with a simpler image from the recent past. When I was a boy, my mother stayed at home to take care of me and my two wicked sisters. My grandmother lived with us, too. This was the norm; all my buddies had moms at home. (Although perhaps not all of them had mothers or grandmothers who washed and dried their hair till they left for college. Ahem. . .) Now, I admit that I am moderately unbalanced as it is, but consider what a nutcase I might have been without all that maternal nurturing.

Today, most mothers work outside of the home. Although this is in large measure due to economic necessity, it is unrealistic to expect that even in more prosperous circumstances women will ever abdicate the freedom of the wide world to return to the tender trap of home. This is just the way things are. Surely no one seriously believes that most kids are better off in day-care centers than with their own parents and grandparents, however flawed. Surely, too, everyone realizes that this social change has had some negative consequences for society as well as for the children themselves. (Just ask any middle-aged teacher how classroom civility in 1990 compares to that of 1960, for instance. I often feel like a wandering Athenian scholar endeavoring to civilize some royal but barbarous Macedonian brats. . .) Finally, however, one must ask, so what? The only route to an ideal world is through the real one. Women are *not* going to march back home. Commercial television is *not* going to be outlawed. And so on. "We are the world," the unwashed sing, and they are. Are you going to erect barriers to keep them out? Ah, that'll only buy some time for your generation but likely not for your children's and definitely not your grandchilren's. You want pleasure? Then, let the underdogs eat cake. You want happiness? Redeem the underdog—and yourselves along with them. In other words, it seems to me that you, the "overdogs"-in-the-making (oh yes you are!), have no honorable alternative but the virtue and grace of selflessness. Will it be easy, or cheap? What do you think? What is, that's worthwhile?

Well, there you have my biases. You now understand why my ideological friends quite rightly consider me thoroughly untrustworthy.

There is yet another pleasure which I derive from speaking to you today, one which will—finally!—bring me at least within hailing distance of a "topic." It is that of redressing a recurring misconception of contemporary social science, that of the primacy of Economic, Political and Psychological Man. This is a grotesque misunderstanding, based largely on readings and misreadings of Marx and Freud, which have consequently trivialized the "explanation" of the most extraordinary human values, gratuitously transforming the sublime into the humdrum. Arthur Koestler describes this as the "magic circle" problem of any "closed system": once you have stepped inside its magic circle, it deprives your critical faculties of any ground to stand on (Koestler 1952).

By focusing on the similarities and differences of East Asia vis-à-vis the larger postmodern world, I hope to trifle just enough with your scholarly worldview that you reexamine the scientism myth and—who knows?—maybe one or two other myths along the way. (You are, I trust, in the mood for a little semi-harmless trifling?) With any luck, I'll at least confuse you. As Krishnamurti puts it, if you expect to make any headway whatsoever in learning, you must start from scratch: you must be willing to question even—especially—those assumptions nearest and dearest to your heart.

One day last week, while enjoying dinner at a favorite Chinese restaraunt, I was reading the *Corpus Christi Caller-Times*. The lead story began, "Yesterday, a visiting expert from a university in L.A. informed a convention of Texas educators that students only fail because of the failure of their teachers and schools." Paraphrasing Confucius, de Tocqueville, and virtually every Greek philosopher worth his salt, I muttered, "Harrumph! If one is not responsible for his failures, then he abdicates all victories as well. How insulting!" Several nearby diners stared. I waved the newspaper in agitation. "The fellow thinks students are as helpless as floppy disks," I exclaimed. Chairs squeaked as they were edged further away from me.

At this moment the waitress brought my house-special fried rice, which contains every vegetable known to China and Texas (excluding okra, thank God). After a few bites, I realized that I had been given *shrimp* fried rice rather than the dish I had ordered. Intolerable. When I complained to the waitresses, the American one said, "Well, you have eaten some and they're the same price, so why don't you just finish this one now?" I stared at her with incredulity. Smiling, wordless, the Chinese waitress scurried away, returning within minutes with an immense platter of the Real McCoy. Later, while waiting to settle my bill at the cash register, I noticed that, although a large sign on the counter clearly proclaimed, "No Checks," the two customers in front of me each paid with a check. Saying only, "Thank you," the Chinese proprietress accepted the bank drafts without question.

Why I bother to mention my typically delicious and reasonable (albeit never cheap) Chinese meal may already be obvious. If not, please forbear the incident as grist to which we'll return after a few additional spins of the hoop of this talk.

It has become axiomatic among most social scientists that the various types of behaviors and ways of thought among the world's peoples are mainly a product of their social, economic, political and psychological circumstances. Two weeks ago, for example, a prominent visiting sociologist proposed, in an unusually thoughtful lecture delivered here on campus, that a communal or group orientation—as opposed to the individualism for which Americans are so noted—is not a function of culture per se but of low economic standing. Well. While socioeconomics clearly plays a role in the outlook and behavior of a group, it is a serious mistake to assume that such a factor is a primary determinant of human affairs. Here is the pertinent section of my written response to Dr. X:

> You attribute a group orientation to low economic status. This is only partly true, I think. May I presume to tease you a bit? Like many—most?—contemporary social scientists, you perhaps forget that political, social, and economic matters are derivative, that is, at the secondary level of the human drama. They stem from the philosophical, theological, scientific and emotional "worldviews" of the world's peoples (paraphrasing Radhakrishnan and Moore). This is not to say that major figures and events at the secondary level—e.g., Karl Marx—cannot have a cybernetic impact on the primary level. They can and do. (Although often, as with Marx, not quite so fundamentally as first seems. . .)  Still, it is clearly at the philosophical/theological/scientific level that we find the ground in which are rooted worldviews, from which spring shoots in the form of values, whose leaves are attitudes and behaviors.

The social scientists' worldview of Economic Man and Psychological Man itself has arisen, I think, as part of a postmodern narcissism of guilt and anxiety, which Christopher Lasch describes as a state of "transcendental self-attention," of "restless, perpetually unsatisfied desire" (1979).   To be postmodern is, as Lasch puts it, to live not for ancestors or offspring but for the moment and for a self which is itself so evanescent as to require constant validation from others.

In Asia we find various cultures in which a group orientation of one sort or another has predominated among virtually all socioeconomic classes. This is most interestingly the case in East Asia, where over many centuries a distinctive worldview has evolved from the day-to-day application of the philosophical, theological and ethical systems of Confucianism, Taoism and Buddhism.   (Throughout this discussion of Chinese ways of thinking I shall be leaning heavily on Professor Wing-Tsit Chan's incomparable *Sourcebook in Chinese Philosophy*.)   The unusually successful and potentially instructive worldview of East Asia, as we shall see, represents a curiously—almost paradoxically—harmonious marriage of seeming opposites: rationality *and* intuition; individual *and* community; randomness *and* order; essence *and* existence; being *and* becoming. In its almost Judaic day-to-day accent on what is manifest rather than on the central but forever-hidden flywheel of the Other, East Asia's point of view and way of life have—again like Judaism—evolved over the course of many centuries with the contributions of many different sages and teachers, from a tradition which respected learning and achievement, but with a considerable dollop of skepticism.

Confucius is the region's touchstone, exemplar and archetype. Anyone who attempts to understand today's China, Korea, Japan or Taiwan without an appreciation of the influence of Confucian assumptions about what constitutes the well-lived life has about as much chance of success as one who would study the United States without comprehending it as a sort of cultural "rainforest," at once both single organism *and* hodgepodge of individualities and differences. (A human being is another good analogy for the U.S.: liver and white blood cells and athlete's-foot fungus, etc., all doing their individual things and simultaneously contributing to the One which transcends all differences.)

Confucius was a Solomon-like sage (although, typically, he denied his own sageness) who lived about five hundred years before Christ. (Calling him a "strange and rather imperious teacher," Bouquet [1962] compares him with the Buddha and John Wesley.) Building on centuries of existing Chinese tradition, Confucius developed a code of personal and social conduct which to a very great degree molded and directed the pattern of later Chinese thought. Unlike the mystics of South Asia, he refused to speak of (the possibility of) God, of "spiritual beings or life after death." His "philosophy"—better thought of as an ethical code—was worldly, practical, realistic and, above all, *humanistic*. Confucius is famous for his emphasis on filial piety and respect for ancestors; for focusing on the worthiness of education ("useful" education at any rate); for his accent on moderation, balance, duty and responsibility; and, finally, for stressing human (not divine) action as the avenue to happiness and success. (Responding to a guru who advised students to fast and meditate all night prior to examinations, Confucius said that in his own experience he did better if he *studied* before his tests. . .) According to Confucius, one's objective should be to become a sagelike, "superior man," a person who exhibits *jen*, a noble, benevolent and altruistic humanity. At first glance, Confucius' thought seems to have been exclusively materialistic and atheistic. Appearances can be deceptive, though, particularly for us Americans, ever ready to believe that what you see is what you get, and that if it walks, looks and quacks like a duck, it must be a duck (see Chapter IV, PopMyth 11).

Confucius was no duck, or at least no simple one. His realistic code of conduct was based on the idealistic premise that humankind is both perfectable and innately good. More importantly, Confucius made it quite clear that *jen* must be rooted in *te*—virtue—which itself depended on the so-called Mandate of Heaven, *t'ien*. This is an essential point. Although Confucius focused on the worldly rather than the otherworldly (recognizing the latter to be unknowable), he made it abundantly clear that the only reason that *te* exists and works in such a way as to permit the coming-into-being of *jen* is that *te* mirrors or resonates the principle which orders—or, perhaps, which *is*—heaven, *t'ien*. (It is said that whenever Confucius was asked about God, he blushed, a sign of respect.)

Although the ordinary focus of Confucianism (and Chinese thought in general) is humanistic, trained on the mundane, worldly, pragmatic level of flesh and blood, it is always understood to require the wisdom which comes only from *t'ien*. To believe that a strictly existential or secular moral system could succeed would be viewed, from a Confucian perspective, as the height of arrogant narcissism, one doomed to certain failure. Such a morality has been described by a Christian moralist as a cut-flower variety, i.e., like a flower separated from its supporting root system, bound to wither. Thus, Confucius, who seems to the casual student the quintessential "secular humanist," would probably have considered the label a contradiction in terms.

Taoism, too, has played a significant role in the development of a distinctly East Asian outlook. Taoism—*Tao* means the "path" or "way" —originated with Lao-Tsu (who like Confucius lived about five or six hundred years before the Christian era) and specifically with his landmark work, the *Tao Te Ching* or "*Book of Changes.*" Where Confucius emphasized "social order and an active, productive life" (Chan 1963), Taoism accents solitude, tranquility, and harmony with the natural order. According to Lao-Tsu and the more mystical Chuang Tsu, the "way" of Tao is "the One, which is natural, eternal, spontaneous, nameless, and indescribable" (ibid.). It is important to recognize that although Taoism emphasizes harmony with nature, it is not a "philosophy of withdrawal. Man is to follow Nature but in doing so he is not eliminated; instead, his nature is fulfilled" (ibid.).

The third major religious influence on East Asian thought, that of Buddhism, began with its initial introduction from India around the beginning of the Christian era, bolstered by a more penetrating injection about the sixth century after Christ. It is difficult to separate the Buddhism that developed in China entirely from Taoism, as they have many parallels and have co-evolved for the past two millennia. However, if Confucianism were to be seen as located at the worldly, pragmatic end of a scale which has Taoism at its center, then, broadly speaking, Buddhism should lie at the opposite, the "other-worldly" end of the Chinese metaphysical spectrum. Whereas in Taoism the objective is unforced action and harmony with nature, the Buddhist seeks a *passionless withdrawal* from this world of ever-changing (i.e., evil) illusions, attachments and suffering.

Ch'an or Zen is the most uniquely East Asian (Chinese and Japanese, respectively) form of Buddhism. In Zen, intensely concentrated meditation is performed in order to achieve *satori*, sudden illumination or enlightenment, i.e., the realization of Nirvana, which is identical with the "Buddha-mind" and, so, with "Buddha-nature" ("suchness" or "thusness"). Although South Asian Buddhists believe the body to be a hindrance to achieving freedom or release, the Chinese and Japanese Buddhists assume that anyone who reaches the

Buddha-nature becomes a Buddha *while in his own body*. Such acceptance—combining the best of philosophical systems—is a peculiarly East Asian (and, especially, Chinese) gift.

(I would be remiss if I failed to acknowledge that the Confucianism, Taoism and Buddhism of popular practice have often been little more than perverted, hollow husks. Too commonly, Confucianism has become a rigid legalism; Taoism, a superstitition long on noise and incense and short on substance; and Buddhism, the unforgivable dogma of Buddha-worship. Let's keep our stones to ourselves, however, for in the religiosity of both Western Christianity and Western scientism we have little to brag about. . .)

As Chinese thought has evolved, beginning particularly with the Neo-Confucianism of around A.D. 1000, it has come increasingly to reflect an all-in-oneness. Neo-Confucianism, beginning with Chou Tun-i, assimilated the Taoist idea of non-being while discarding Taoism's fantasy and mysticism, with which the Chinese character was never fully in harmony. Chou Tun-i said that "the many are ultimately one, and the one is actually differentiated into the many," and that "the one and many each has its own correct state of being" (Chan 1963). He further emphasized the importance of principle (*li*), of nature, of destiny, and of a sincerity (*ch'eng*) which is the foundation of moral nature and the source of all activities (ibid.).

More than in any other world culture, East Asians came to consider themselves not just Confucian or Taoist or Buddhist but all three simultaneously. Hence the peculiar combination of the worldly, practical and collective on one level, the individual, tranquil and harmonious on another, and a retreat into transcendence on yet another.

It is quite correct that East Asia's philosophical all-in-oneness, or "plural belonging" (Bouquet 1962), can appear to have ended when confronted with the Marxism and materialism of the twentieth century. Today, after a half-century of Marxist doctrine, relatively few Chinese identify themselves with any of these creeds, and many reject them. In contemporary Japan as well, many people—perhaps most—are no longer practicing Buddhists, Confucianists or Shintoists, except at ceremonial events like funerals and weddings. Once more, however, we must be wary of the simplicity of easy impressions. Scratch at the surface of a Minnesotan in the 1990s and—professed religion notwithstanding—you're still likely to discover the social code of Garrison Keillor's Lake Wobegon, that is, a Nordic/Germanic/Lutheran worldview which includes the virtue, meaning and necessity of hard work by responsible individuals. So, too, East Asians remain deeply influenced, however unconsciously, by two and one-half millennia of Confucianism and Taoism and many centuries of Buddhism. The result is a synthetic outlook which manages to accommodate such seeming opposites as the self and the collectivity; form and function; idea and substance; essence and existence; being and doing. Hence the relevance of a typical Chinese meal, such as that to which I earlier referred, where this unique, many-in-one attitudinal admixture unselfconsciously manifests itself to eye, ear, and palate.

Neils Bohr, the quantum physicist, suggested that postmodern science will have to be complementary, an idea he apparently borrowed from Søren Kierkegaard. *Complementarity* suggests that different, even contradictory explanations of some phenomena may be equally valid, and further, that through such reconciliation a higher degree of understanding may be achieved. This unfolding Western paradigm shift, possibly the most significant change in the dominant mode of thought in the West since Copernicus (Barzun 1989), has I suggest been anticipated in the syncretism of East Asia: the capacity to hold apparently mutually exclusive beliefs simultaneously is as fundamentally Chinese as the Yellow River. So also is the implementation within one's personal reality of the doctrine of the unity of Human and Heavenly Nature (Bouquet 1962).

How else to explain the "economic miracle" of Japan and the "four little dragons" of Taiwan, South Korea, Hong Kong and Singapore, or of the material success of the "overseas Chinese" and other East Asians? In the U.S., the average IQ of Asian-Americans is eight points higher than the general mean, and in various technical and professional advanced-degree programs Asians and Asian-Americans comprise fifty percent or more of the classes, far beyond their proportion in the population at large. Surely we are not such racists as to believe that young East Asians are simply born into smarter families than everyone else. What they *are* born into is a philosophical system which links them all to the One from which they come by connecting "success" to *jen, te* and, finally, to a *t'ien* so long-forgotten, so long-honored that their relation to it has become autonomic, like breathing. Born, in other words, into a worldly set of values (where the rational, consciously constructed life of action and accomplishment is central and dominates day-to-day life) together with the intuitive, "felt" foundation of harmony and significance on which worldly life rests.

A recent survey (Raeburn 1991) asked Japanese adults to rank those aspects of their country of which they were most proud. The results are instructive. They rated maintenance of social order at the top; following, in order, were: natural beauty; history and traditions; diligence and talent of the people; a high level of education; national prosperity; culture and the arts; and, finally, science and technology. It is interesting to speculate about how adults in the United States would respond to a similar survey. . .

In the *Book of Changes* it is said that "in the world there are many different roads but the destination is the same" (Chan 1963). Consider also the following passage from "The Doctrine of the Mean," an eight-hundred-year-old discourse on human nature and metaphysics (one of the "classics" on which were based the Chinese civil service exams between 1313 and 1905):

Therefore absolute sincerity is ceaseless. Being ceaseless, it is lasting. Being lasting, it is evident. Being evident, it is infinite. Being infinite, it is extensive and deep. Being extensive and deep, it is high and brilliant. It is because it is extensive and deep that it contains all things. It is because it is high and brilliant that it overshadows all things. It is because it is infinite and lasting that it can complete all things. In being extensive and deep, it is a counterpart of Earth. In being high and brilliant, it is a counterpart of Heaven. In being infinite and lasting, it is unlimited. Such being its nature, it becomes prominent without any display, produces changes without motion, and accomplishes its ends without action. (Chan 1963)

Last Thursday, I took my family to Vattmann, Texas, for that community's annual Thanksgiving public "feed." As usual, Highway 77 was a nightmare. (My daughter arrived an hour late because of several monumental wrecks between Victoria and Corpus Christi.) Every third car was weaving frantically from lane to lane, narrowly missing other vehicles. Some of us drove at 55 MPH, more of us at 85, everyone else somewhere in between. Meanwhile, cars approaching from side roads pulled into the relentless traffic as though seeking the sudden enlightenment which comes with merger into the Greater Truth of an eighteen-wheeler.

As we proceeded south from Kingsville, we joined a caravan of thousands heading toward the Valley, all doubtless anxious to share the holiday with a community of friends and family. Ironically, however, on Highway 77 there was none of the assumed social code, structure or even civility of "community." Nor was this frenzy a sign of old-fashioned, American rugged individualism either, for genuine individualism requires the observation of one sacrosanct rule: I respect you, you respect me. These days, we're beyond all such constraints, all limits, all rules. Block the fast lane at a mere 55 MPH and those of us behind wave our fists, or tire irons, or worse, and scream, "Get a life, shtupuk!" (I trust none of you speaks Serbo-Croatian.) As Max Picard puts it,

In the modern world the individual no longer faces silence, no longer faces the community, but faces only the universal noise. The individual stands between noise and silence. He is isolated from noise and isolated from silence. He is forlorn. (1952)

This, postmodernity's darkest face, is *solipsism*, that philosophy of ultimate despair and anger in which the tribe's collectivity has become inauthentic, as has the autonomous but responsible individual of modernity. The only remaining reality is that of narcissism: me. Or is it? Being requires boundary, Martin Heidegger said someplace. The spectre which haunts the postmodern person is the suspicion that finally I, too, am illusion.

For most of this century Western social scientists assumed that world cultures were converging, becoming more and more homogeneous in the ubiquity and dominance of television and such other EuroAmerican "stuff" as

Levis, English, rock'n'roll and hamburgers. This view turned out to underestimate both the tenacity and the merits of cultural differences, and so in recent decades, our social thinkers have shifted to accenting the importance of diversity and pluralism. By itself, however, this theme is just as unsatisfying.

What we are beginning to witness I think is the convergence of "modern" separateness with "primitive" connectedness. If so, this is a very hopeful sign, for the lesson of Highway 77 is that neither the former nor the latter can be sustained for long in the absence of the other. Consider, to recall one of Simone Weil's dictums, how worthless are individual "rights" without a sense of personal responsibility.

Western Europe, and California, perhaps, are in the late twentieth century beginning to exhibit an odd, ad hoc sociophilosophical evolution toward a celebration of difference played out on a collective stage whose props are those of shared assumptions regarding the good material life; namely, assumptions that the good life is attainable; that it is worthwhile; that it sometimes requires the submission of the individual will to that of the organism; and that otherwise, "anything goes." I believe that this attitude may well represent a first step toward a neomodern, neo-Western complementarity of such "opposing" values as striving and contentedness, hierarchy and equality, the absolute and the relative.

Two vital questions remain to be answered during your lifetimes. Firstly, good quasi-Neo-Confucian that I am, I believe that a successful humanism has to be rooted in a *jen*, humanity, resting on the bedrock of *te*, virtue, which in turn exists only because of the Mandate of Heaven, *t'ien*. How the evolving neo-Western worldview will reconnect *te* and *t'ien* is unclear. But without some manner of linkage between existence and essence, chaos and cosmos, the center of the new episteme will not hold, and it too will fall apart. Witness the failure of the Marxist attempt at a strictly existential union of theory and practice, that is, of *te* and *jen*. And, in spite of the undeniable attractiveness of the current argument that modernity has forced history and nature itself—and so the very idea of "centers"—to disappear "through the skylight" (Hardison 1989), the moral of East Asia's story is that *both* the thingless, ceaseless flux *and* the thingliness which continuously expresses the flux are worthy. Dostoevsky claimed that Man can preserve his human form only so long as he believes in God (Picard 1952). If one is willing to substitute "the transcendent" or even "the Other" for Dostoevsky's "God," perhaps the highest lesson we may draw from East Asia is that Dostoevsky was correct (i.e., that mankind can be human only through faith in God), and finding the connections between *am* and *am not* is the first vital challenge of our times.

Secondly, what of the rest of the postmodern world? Even if Europe and California and East Asia do manage to harmonize those twin anthems—constancy and change—which together now appear to shape both cosmic and human patterns, what of all those places where we sometimes seem to be witnessing the worst possible amalgamation of tribalism with solipsism?

With your permission, I shall respond with several little vignettes. In August, after returning from a prolonged visit to the Middle East, I rejoined my department's coffee club. When I brought several pounds of coffee as my share for August but not June or July (when I was out of the country), another member—not known for selfless interests—posted a very visible notice demanding that every member contribute every month, regardless of his or her presence on campus. This, the facile, public sentimentality of kitsch, leaves me cold, for the illusion of concern offers no more substance than does cotton candy.

Ten days ago, I received a call from a student in one of my beginning science classes. This student is frequently absent, leaves class early, reads romance novels during my lectures, and has flunked two of the last three exams. As she is clearly intelligent, her failure is the worst sort, that of uncaring sloth. Could she attend a different lab session that week, she wanted to know, so that she could leave campus a day early that week? "Well," I replied, "not this late in the term, because the labs progress at varying rates depending on the rates at which students progress. The other lab will not be dealing with the same material as will yours." "Oh," she said, exasperated, "you are so unfair. All I want is credit for attending the lab!"

The day prior to Thanksgiving I found myself in one of those endless holiday lines for which the local supermarket is infamous. Pulling her cart behind her, the lady in front of me emptied her purchases onto the check-out counter. While the rest of us waited, she sent several kiddies running to retrieve some candy and cigarettes. When the clerk had rung up a total, she had yet to begin even searching for her checkbook, much less actually writing the draft. Finally, leaving my way blocked by her abandoned cart, she began strolling away. "Excuse me, ma'am," I called, affecting a smile. "Your cart?" "Huh?" She replied. She glanced at the offending implement. "Nah." And out she went.

Saturday, I was reading the November issue of *NEA Today*, the monthly newspaper of the National Educational Association, the largest American teachers' organization. The following item was reported, with obvious approval:

A few Bethlemem [?] Pa. parents are suing their school system over a new program requiring students to perform 60 hours of volunteer work over four years. [This is slightly more than one hour per month.] "I don't want my son to be told what to do," said one parent. "I went to school in free America, and I want the same for my children." (1990)

Last week my wife, an industrial technology teacher in a local high school, told me a disturbing story. It seems that recently, in a small-town high school not far from Kingsville, one young ruffian beat another boy into a state of permanent paralysis. Three teachers witnessed the incident but did not attempt to intervene. The principal and assistant principal were summoned but apparently refused to come to the scene. One can only speculate as to just how much time had elapsed by the time the police finally arrived. My wife was told this story by her colleagues, many of whom defended the teachers who watched the student being thrashed into a lifetime of paralysis. "The kid may have had a knife," they argued. "We're teachers, not bouncers. That's not my job!" At this stage in her story, my wife, a product of the union of an East Texas Baptist and a middle-western German-Catholic, looked at me and, echoing Confucius, said, "Life at such a cost is too expensive."

Lastly, following is an excerpt from a letter from a Haitian friend of a friend, who had just returned to Canada after a brief attempt to teach back in Haiti:

> As a returning Haitian, I found that my presence was very disturbing to the middle-class establishment. After living more than eighteen years in North America, I had internalized such values as human equality, the work ethic, individual freedom, fairness, sense of the public good. And here I was in a society built precisely on the opposite values, having to confront, every day, the ethos of the Haitian middle class, the result of a long colonial history, crystallized through the social conditioning carried on for thirty years by the dictatorial regime of the Duvaliers. You wouldn't believe the social pressure brought to bear upon the individual to accept the tenets of the middle-class ethos. To live in Haiti, you have to put a dimmer on your intelligence and kill your conscience, agreeing that corruption is and should be the norm, that inequality is and should be the organizing principle of society and basis of social relations, that stealing is better than working, that narrowly self-centered interest should prevail over the common good.
>
> Returning Haitians, willy-nilly, are perceived as bearers of modernity and the values of liberal democracy. As such, they are implicit critics of the slave plantation value-system that underlies so much of contemporary Haitian society and culture. Eminently threatening to the status quo, they are to be ostracized or eliminated, yes, physically. In the end, then, for the salvation of my soul and my physical integrity, I had to leave. . .
>
> I had to leave, for the changes needed within Haitian society are of a deeper nature than the mere organization of elections and the creation of institutions superficially democratic. I was told a horrible story in Haiti, whose mythic character expresses both Haitians' perception of themselves and their understanding of the quality of the social relations that prevail in Haiti, of the kind of rapports between individual and society as well as among individuals. One day, God invited every nation to send Him two representatives. Whatever the first representative of a nation would ask Him, He would grant to him/her, but He would give twice as much to the second representative. Thus, to the first American, He gave one million dollars and to the second American two million. He gave literary fame all over France to the first Frenchman, and fame all over Europe to the second Frenchman.

When came the turn of the Haitian delegates, the first Haitian glanced sideways at his countryman and said to God, "Lord, I want you to blind me in one eye, to cripple one of my arms and to cut off one of my legs." Thus, the illuminating truth of the myth points to the deeper, darker impulses that too often inspire our actions, behaviors, to the point of rendering us unable to apply ourselves to any collective endeavor, even for our collective salvation. . .

So, you see, my presence is quite irrelevant. And if there was any hesitation on my part to go North, my decision became unshakable the night my apartment block was besieged and the residence of my landlady next door invaded by gun-shooting former tonton-macoutes.

Yi-Fu Tuan quotes Anatoly Sobchak, mayor of Leningrad, as telling the following folk tale about the problem of jealousy and resentment in the Soviet Union:

> God comes to a lucky Russian peasant one day and offers him any wish in the world. The peasant is excited and starts dreaming his fantasies. "Just remember," God says, "whatever you choose, I will do twice as much for your neighbor as I do for you." The peasant is stumped because he cannot bear to think of his neighbor being so much better off than he is, no matter how well off he becomes. Finally, he gets an idea and tells God, "Strike out one of my eyes and take out both eyes of my neighbor." (Tuan 1990a)

These eerily parallel stories of the Haitian's and the Russian's requests that they be crippled to make their compatriots doubly so would today, sadly, ring just as true in (for example) Yugoslavia, Sri Lanka, Kashmir, Myanmar (Burma), Liberia, Peru, and, several of the Soviet "republics" of Central Asia. What of the future South Texas?

The answer to this, and to the questions I posed earlier, will be written by you and your kind. Perhaps you still believe that you are here only to acquire a modicum of information and a few job skills? Not so. Your true assignment, should you choose to accept it, is merely to redeem the world—or your part of it, anyhow—through the example of your lives. You are the sages-in-training. Alas, I must in good conscience warn you not only that wisdom's way is one whose horizon is ever receding, but also that most of the great sages of the past ended up broke and broken, convinced by the preponderance of evidence all about them that they had failed to have much impact.

But, then, resolving these problems is not part of your job description. They'll be decided in *t'ien*. Take it from an aging quasi-Neo-Confucian: the tao of genuine virtue, born of the grace of gratitude, leads to happiness here and, I suspect, to *t'ien* itself.

Bon voyage.

## Review and Reflections on the Text

1.    Define *jen*; *te* and *t'ien*; *li*; *ch'eng*; complementarity.

2.    Reflect on the idea that faith is a submission to the duality of beauty and horror.  Write a paragraph about an event or experience in which you have recognized both qualities.

3.    In what sense is Confucianism secular in its emphasis?  Why might Confucius be confused by the term "secular humanism"?

4.    What is the central quest of Buddhism?  How does the Buddhism of East Asia differ from that of South Asia?

5.    Considering the author's comments on Confucianism, Taoism, and Buddhism, review the anecdote about lunch at the Chinese restaurant.  How do the various parts of that meal demonstrate a Neo-Confucian blend of attitudes?

6.    Examine the results of the survey on how Japanese people rank their reasons for pride in their country.  How would you rank these same elements for the United States?  Would you add other elements that are important to your sense of pride in the U.S.?  As a class project, conduct a similar survey around your campus or community and analyze the results for what they indicate about basic cultural values.

7.    What in highway holiday traffic behavior demonstrates solipsism?  How is solipsism different from individualism?  Recall incidents or events within your own experience or knowledge that reflect solipsistic attitudes or an "amalgamation of tribalism with solipsism."  How do you feel about them?

8.    What are the "two vital questions" the author says "remain to be answered during your lifetimes."  What kinds of activity, both individual and collective, do you think will help resolve these problems?

# VI. The Fourth Paradigm<sup>*</sup>

"Going to the Feelies this evening, Henry?" enquired the Assistant Predestinator. "I hear the new one at the Alhambra is first-rate. There's a love scene on a bearskin rug; they say it's marvellous. Every hair of the bear reproduced. The most amazing tactual effects."
—Aldous Huxley, *Brave New World*

Substance of objects is something; we know not what.
—John Locke, *An Essay Concerning Human Understanding*

Hello. Permit me to preface my remarks with a celebration of your perspicacious selection of teachers. Even in the university—a cynic might say, especially in the university!—one encounters commonplace minds at the helms of some of the intellectual voyages of discovery, as you have doubtless found. Competent enough at the basic, informational level of learning (two plus two equals four, Columbus sailed the ocean blue in 1492, and so on), these factualist pedants are, at best, apprentices. Let us be kind and call them "instructors."

Further up the knowledge pyramid than the factualists there are those of us who deal in the marketplace of ideas, but because ideas are merely by-products of thinking, we literalists are really only synthesists. We have reached a certain level of competence but we are not yet true thinkers for we do not create the ideas we trade in. We are the "professors." We have had impressive formal titles conferred upon us by academic authorities. Our interest in concepts is sincere, we work (fairly) hard, we retain much of what we have studied, we are often erudite and occasionally brilliant. Still, ours is the realm of noise rather than silence, and—other than the odd, momentary

<sup>*</sup>A guest lecture delivered on March 8, 1991, to a senior-level political science class, "Society and Technology," team-taught by Professors Robert Davidson and Sandy Hicks.

misgiving—we do not yet comprehend the limitless vistas of our ignorance. (Geographer Ian Burton said not long ago that the learned are always oppressed by a sense of growing stupidity for, as islands of knowledge rise higher, their boundaries with the sea of ignorance are forever *expanding* [1991].)

There are among us, however, a precious few helmsmen who venture into the very realm of thinking. Sophocles described theirs as "the power that crosses the white sea making a path under surges that threaten to engulf [them]" (quoted by Stonebarger 1985). Far above mere synthesis, this is the stratum of analysis and discrimination and, thus, creativity. Here, and only here, is the concentrated mastery (once called "genius") of true *teachers*. True teachers are reconciled to the terribly finite nature of what they know. Consequently, unlike the rest of us pedagogues, these few listen and are comfortable in the world of silence. Nevertheless, because enlightenment lies as much in community as in solitude, the world of noise—where else to find students?—is theirs, too.

True teachers must also be true believers. To pursue what Saint Augustine felicitously termed the "light of the source of reason," which is what education is finally all about, one must have faith that such absolute qualities as truth, beauty, goodness, and quality itself either exist in reality or at least exist as potentialities awaiting investiture by conscious intelligence. The authentic teacher, like the genuine scholar, may as often conceive of herself as *seeking* the source of the primary qualities, like goodness, wisdom and compassion (the essentialist quest), as *creating* them existentially; but cynicism is by definition beyond her pale.

You are privileged to be regularly in the presence of two such sherpas. I am envious.

Well. Perhaps we should push on before our colloquy becomes a eulogy.

In any period, attitudes concerning *the* appropriate relationship between humans and their environments reflect existing conceptions ("knowledge") of the character and meaning of existence. Such understandings are reached via two avenues. The first is the path of reason or logic, the other that of intuition or instinct. Composing this lecture, for example, I endeavored to think rationally or logically, whereas a spider weaves her web instinctively. Each of these methods, however, may exhibit its own kind of knowledge, and I shall need both in plenty this morning, for I hope to transport you to a realm a friend once scornfully dismissed as "romantic science."

Fear not: you'll be in fine company. Loren Eiseley, the most lyrical naturalist of his time, once passed up a promising archaeological site in order to avoid disturbing the nestlings of a rare eagle. His rationale was something like: Oh well, it was foolish but I'm happy for I *did right by life* in the sight of the universe (1946). Romantic science demands a naive faith in meaning and mystery. Listen, for example, to the very crusty, very naive, G. K. Chesterton:

> The only words that ever satisfied me as describing Nature are the terms used in the fairy books, "charm," "spell," "enchantment." They express the arbitrariness of the fact and its mystery. A tree grows fruit because it is bewitched. The sun shines because it is bewitched. (1926)

Truth is something quite different from factual knowledge, if by Truth we mean ultimate reality. Truth in this sense is much less accessible than mere accurate information or "true knowledge" (Heller 1990), which is not wrong so much as it is incomplete and therefore strictly provisional. Kenneth Boulding once described mathematics as "rather elaborate glimpses of the obvious" (1980), exemplifying at once both "true knowledge" (mathematics) and Truth (the obvious, after the fact). If you ask me to describe Mother Teresa of Calcutta, I might reply that she is a fast-decaying assemblage of biomass totaling 97.359 pounds. (I might even mention that she gave up a promising career as a geography teacher. . .) So what? True knowledge may in other words be so terribly incomplete as to constitute a kind of fabrication. Melville begins *Moby-Dick* with the definition given by the nineteenth-century French naturalist George Cuvier, "The Whale is a mammiferous animal without hind feet." Precision posing as accuracy invariably takes one farther from Truth than an answer such as (in Mother Teresa's case) "I cannot describe her," or even "a saint."

People seem almost universally to exhibit what David Hume terms "natural belief" in Truth (E. L. Miller 1972). The extent to which we may enter the realm of Truth is debatable. Chinese tradition argues for the existence of *wu-wei* or "no-knowledge," an unforced harmony with Tao, the way of ultimate reality. Hindus and Buddhists (and followers of mysticism in general) claim that access to "wisdom without understanding" (as Saint John of the Cross described it) is possible via retreat into contemplation or meditation. The ancient Hindu *Mandukya Upanishad* claims such wisdom is "beyond the senses, beyond the understanding, beyond all expression. [It] is pure unitary consciousness, wherein awareness of the world and of multiplicity is . . . obliterated" (quoted in E. L. Miller 1972).

In the West, breakthroughs to such wisdom are sometimes ascribed to poets, artists and musicians. Max Picard, for example, has said that it is only in the language of poets that the *real* word, the word connected with silence—i.e., the Absolute—still sometimes appears (1952). We can't resolve this question here today but it is a vital one, for as John Garvey expressed it, "no one but a serious disciple of Oscar Wilde would consciously prefer the counterfeit to the real" (1991).

Just as one might think of Mother T. as ninety-seven pounds of matter, it is quite possible to discern the universe—or one's neighborhood—as a nothing more than so much stuff. It is in fact this perspective of Nature, of everything, as absolutely gratuitous and thus meaningless that has come to dominante in the West. According both to prevailing philosophical viewpoints and to the pop existentialism of Bart Simpson et al., there is no mystery whatsoever to the phenomenal world—it simply "is," man, no big deal—and no Truth lies above, beyond or behind phenomenal existence itself.

A second and, historically, equally important foundation of Western thought has been the essentialist tradition. According to this Platonic/Kantian view, the phenomenal world of observable things is a secondary or derivative one which masks the far truer *noumenal* realm. This, the world as it "truly is" (as opposed to the world of mere sensory perception), is the Platonic realm of ideal forms, i.e., of ultimate reality or Truth, which lies beyond the reach of the physical senses.

I am informed that many of you are students of engineering and the natural sciences. If so, you may by habit or inclination find yourselves predisposed toward phenomenal "true knowledge" rather than Plato's noumenal "Truth." I myself find, say, that sudden actual contact of my foot with the reality of my bedframe registers with me in a way that the pure idea of a stubbed toe does not. And, no matter how convinced I may be in principle of the University's gratitude for the quality of my work, in some very fundamental way a raise in my salary somehow means more.

The character of contemporary life is such that, in our ordinary, day-to-day experiences—excepting moments of emotional, physical and spiritual crisis—most of us think and act in this way most of the time. We take life, awareness, and all of existence for granted, as unremarkable as catsup on a cheeseburger. This was driven home to me several years ago by a Riviera (Texas) middle-schooler who, commenting on the values of his generation, noted, "If we can't eat it, wear it, or drive it, it doesn't exist, man!"

Western technology rests on the abiding faith of scientists and engineers that the universe makes sense according to a few simple, orderly, underlying patterns and, further, that human beings can, to a point, discern these patterns and so comprehend the nature of Nature. For example, we presume that gravity does not become quixotic on, say, Saturdays or on Christmas Eves but works the same way day in and day out. We also trust (I use the term advisedly) that gravity is *not* totally beyond the pale of human understanding.

However, first modern and now postmodern science (e.g., quantum physics) has revealed the quintessential fuzziness of Nature. In this universe, what you (seem to) see is not necessarily what you get. Auroras, the sky's blue color, the sky itself for that matter, begin on close inspection to resemble phantoms invoked by the interplay of air and sunlight more than objective actualities. My lectern here seems considerably more substantial, more demonstrable, far truer than does an abstract quality like, let us say, "quality" itself, but is it? As science students, you all know perfectly well that the seeming solidity of my podium is an illusion fostered by the electromagnetic force-fields binding its matter together. And by now it has become a grade-school truism that Democritus' billiard-ball-like atoms *themselves* consist of space and yet more space and, here and there, subatomic particles which finally begin to resemble nothing so much as concentrated assemblages or vortices of light. In other words, fundamental distinctions like energy versus matter or living versus nonliving begin consistently to look more like permeable membranes than like singular chasmlike divides. At the least, they have become very much less clear than we once believed. What point—somewhere between virus and amoeba?—is the threshold which separates "life" from the rest of nature? What, finally, divides matter from energy? Here was Thomas Mann's prescient response to such unanswerables:

> Life, which had been called forth from Being just as Being had been from Nothingness—Life, this fine flower of Being—consisted of the same raw material as inanimate Nature. . . One could not even say it was unambiguously distinguishable from simple Being. Always when Nature produced the deceptive appearance of the organic in the inorganic . . . she was trying to teach us that she was one. (Mann 1955)

Moreover, in addition to being fuzzy, Nature turns out to be a remarkably capricious place. Like Einstein, most of us have presumed that "God does not play dice" with the universe; in other words, given enough true information about any system, one could predict perfectly its behavior. But we now know that this faith was misplaced. Of a block of radium 226, which specific particles will decay in the next 1620 years, and which will not? One cannot say, for by definition one cannot predict the occurrence of accidental events. And if this is true of physical systems, then it is likely that biological, social and psychological systems must be even less predictable. Randomness, uncertainty, and complexity of this sort appear so commonplace, so thoroughly part of the warp and woof of existence, that the universe now seems as much chaos as cosmos.

Yet, Nature's dance can be described by mathematical equations. The equations' descriptions are crude, true. That's hardly a surprise. What is remarkable, and what suggests that they are much more than the mere solipsistic projections we too often take for truth, is that they *work*. Thus, the larger rhythms of existence are those of the order and simplicity of cosmos. If the comprehensibility of Nature was the great mystery for *modern* science as Einstein claimed (Ferris 1985), *postmodern* science's great paradox is that of a universe that is both simple and complex, simultaneously.

Over the years, I recall hearing each of your professors—sorry, "teachers"!—saying, in effect, "On Monday, Wednesday, and Friday I'm an essentialist but on Tuesdays, Thursdays and Saturdays, an existentialist." (One presumes that even such as they rest on Sunday...) Thus, they anticipate the new worldview, what I call the fourth great sociophilosophical paradigm, that of syncretism based on the principle of *complementarity*.

The idea of complementarity owes to the Christian existential philosopher Søren Kierkegaard and to the early quantum physicist Neils Bohr. According to this idea, opposing explanations not only are sometimes equally valid (e.g., light is either wavelike or particlelike, depending on your experiment) but are both necessary for the fullest understanding.

Until the revolutionary advent of the postmodern sciences in the past half-century (e.g., quantum physics and the sciences of nonlinear, chaotic systems such as the atmosphere and of complex adaptive or self-organizational systems), the history of Western thought reflected the evolution of three great worldviews or paradigms regarding Nature and humankind's place in it. *Rationality* arose several centuries before the Christian era among such Greek thinkers as Plato, Anaximander, Democritus, Erastosthanes and, *The* Philosopher, Aristotle, replacing an earlier *mythological* order wherein primitive people experienced a sense of mystical participation with the natural and supernatural worlds (P. L. Berger 1981). The new outlook of the "Hellenic rupture" saw a world that was best addressed through autonomous reason (especially with the *why* questions) rather than through magic, superstition or the experience of cosmic participation. Then, sixteen or seventeen centuries ago, a *religious* perspective of existence arose and came to dominate, one whose worldly aspect was seen through a lens of faith in The (not "an") Other.[1]

The *scientific* worldview, which exploded onto the scene as the noosphere of Copernicus, Newton, Galileo, Kant, Descartes et al., assumed a single, unified *cosmos* (an idea borrowed from the Judeo-Christian-Islamic tradition). It posited that empirical "true knowledge" (sense-information) alone could eventually answer every question about Truth (except, perhaps, the Greek *why?*). Its comprehension of an orderly, explicable field of existence reached its culmination in Einstein, whose daring naivete ($E=mc^2$) unwittingly led to its demise.

Why did the scientific worldview enjoy such fantastic success? That one's easy: it worked. From radar, polio vaccine, laser printers, contact lenses and gyroscopes to microchips, call forwarding, slinkies and, shortly, 3-D holovision, modernity's virtual universe (pardon the pun) of technical marvels owes to a scientific paradigm in which true knowledge has been gained, in Kenneth Boulding's acute phrase, through "the orderly detection of error" (1980).

Each of the first two of these great Western worldviews were, in their turn, found wanting. More accurately, each came to be viewed as equally ingenious and ingenuous, well intended but simple minded.

Now, in this century, the scientific paradigm too has finally reached its limits. Let's take a moment to consider why and how this happened.

Nature is an ongoing process, a series of often (maybe usually) random fluxes, ephemeral whirls in a ceaseless torrent.

> All things are in flux, in agitation, everything overlaps and joins with everything else. Even abstractions sweat and grow dishevelled. Nothing is motionless. There is no isolation. Only activity, concentrated activity: form. (Cendrars 1970)

As Heraclitus said over twenty centuries ago, you cannot step into the same river twice, for both you and the stream have changed.

Yet, in some fundamental way, the stream *is*. Whether its most elemental nature is "essence" or "existence" is a question of Truth and so presently, perhaps forever, beyond the ken of rational inquiry. Intuition—with a pinch of no-knowledge (*wu-wei*), maybe—suggests to many of us that the equally profound, seemingly intrinsic duality of Nature's *beauty* on the one hand and its awful *power* on the other are at some unplumbed depth reconciled. Perhaps essence and existence are also. In the words of John Locke quoted at the beginning of this essay, "Substance of objects is something; we know not what."

Contemporary philosophers and social scientists frequently claim the "disappearance" of Nature—as well as that of history, philosophy, human nature itself, and even (horrors!) geography (a current pop deconstructionist article on computer networking speaks disdainfully of the "irrelevance of geography" [Branwyn 1991])—arguing that because all our conceptions of the universe and of anything else are self-created (i.e., artificial) and beyond verification, they have no significance beyond themselves. True knowledge speaks only of and to other true knowledge, never of Truth. Fair enough. This is modernity in bravest, fullest flower, "the ongoing concretization of freedom," in Hegel's lovely phrase (quoted by Heller 1990). Because the ultimate reality of Truth is likely always to be in some measure Other, our understanding of it inevitably seems to lie on the far side of an ever-receding horizon. Imagine, for instance, a small vortex in a stream somehow able to contemplate the constant inconstancy of all the other fluxes—currents, eddies, waves, whirls, tides—of which it is a part. But this quandary is not without its appealing aspect. After all, "if things were due to man's creation, we would know them absolutely in language" (Picard 1952) and then what would we do with our sense of wonder?

The metaphoric disappearance of Nature is a postmodern consciousness which reflects and signifies a new, emerging worldview. The field of space/time of which we thinking vortices are a (very!) temporary part is neither essence nor existence (in our old way of considering such) but an ongoing, unfolding process.

It is important to observe that saying this is by no means the same as arguing that Nature has *literally* disappeared. This grievous error recurs mainly among disaffected humanists and social scientists who, having discovered to their dismay that the patterns of natural systems often seem more chaotic than like the products of orderly, mechanical laws, have discarded not merely the naive assumption that such patterns could prove perfectly explicable and predictable but also the very phenomena they had set out to comprehend.

This mistake is as terrible as it is wholly gratuitous. It is terrible because, as Dostoevsky said, a worldview that denies any coherence in the universe—one that posits an arbitrary fate as the sole determinant—is a prescription for personal and social catastrophe (Jackson 1981). Put another way, to deny all underlying symmetry is to invalidate the elemental human values like love, loyalty, and faith (Picard 1952) because what inspires both individual worth and social duty is the perceived honor of being a human, of being a person of honor:

> "Honor" here means knowing how little one brings and how much one has received, and feeling impelled to discharge the debt. Since repaying ancestors is not possible, neighbors and descendants become our natural creditors. To be sure, for those who live without history there are no ancestors to repay. And it is doubtless less agreeable to think of debts than to think of rights, which serve our needs incessantly and so make us by instinct rights advocates. But anyone who claims the fundamental right of equality—the right to every other right—is culpable if he does not know and feel that Equality implies Reciprocity. To enjoy rights without making a return is the game of the usurper and despoiler.
>
> In a high civilization the things that satisfy our innumerable desires look as if they were supplied automatically, mechanically, so that nothing is owed to particular persons; goods belong by congenital right to anybody who takes the trouble to be born. This is the infant's normal greed prolonged into adult life and headed for retribution. When sufficiently general, the habit of grabbing, cheating, and evading reciprocity is the best way to degrade a civilization, and perhaps bring about its collapse. (Barzun 1990)

The error is gratuitous as well because, while the universe is not *wholly* coherent (why should it be?), it not only does not lack coherencies, its patterns seem likely to be at least as fundamental as its incoherencies. I refer to what Kenneth Boulding has termed "the great regularities," about which any good kindergarten teacher could fill a tome. (Even *my* fast-aging bones, for instance, are invulnerable to the attack of any number of words per se, but a few sticks and stones could fracture every bone in my body.) So while it is quite correct that you can't step into the same river twice, it is likely that the next river will

be as cool and refreshing as the last (Bateson 1979). Patterns—strange attrac-
tors, if you wish—do exist.

The belief that Truth not only is unknowable but doesn't exist (other
than in cynical, ironic and relativistic versions, e.g., "*Sure* Santa Claus exists,
Virginia") is nothing less than postexistential superstition. Magic. Sleight-of-
mind, slight-of-soul.   One recalls Max Picard's comment on the world of
"radio-noise":

> It seems like a world of magic, for everything takes place in it without human
> decision, of its own accord. And precisely this appearance of magic is what seduces
> man. (Picard 1952)

Thus is modernity's relentless dialectic with the mystery of a universe
of wonders replaced by the magic of a self-love (i.e., the invocation "*my* will
be done") raised to contempt for the Real—and that is the great danger of
modern solipsism.   One fears that solipsism as a paradigmatic self- and
worldview is fast becoming what Arthur Koestler (borrowing from the fabulist
Jacob Grimm, I believe) termed a "magic circle":

> Once you have stepped within the framework of absolute claims and assumptions
> which together comprise a "closed [sociophilosophical] system"—Marxism and
> Freudianism are favorite Koestlerian examples of magic circles—it deprives your
> critical faculties of any ground to stand on. (Levene 1984 citing Koestler 1952)

Consider this telling bit of free verse from postmodernist critic Ihab
Hassan:

> The theme of this
> > paracritical essay
>
> > > > is        the growing
> > > > insistence of Mind
>
> > to apprehend reality im-mediately
> > to gather more and more mind
>
> > > > in itself;
> > > > thus to become
> > > > its own
> > > > reality(.)
>
> > > > > (1975, reprinted in Conner 1989)

Let us examine for a moment an orange or, more accurately, that
temporary but tasty particularity I choose to call "orange."  (Stage directions:
Hold up particularly nice specimens.  Pass one around.)  Does "orange" or

"naranja"—or "Moe," "Curley" or "Larry," for that matter—correspond in any significant way to the ultimate reality of the thing-in-itself that I refer to as "orange"? Of course not. One is free to choose from limitless possibilities. The treacherous bridge between sign and thing is as ethereal, as elusive, and as rent with voids as a B-movie ghost. One who ventures to cross the void may at any moment plunge down to—what?—meaninglessness at any moment.

(I am unwilling to concede that the bridge is entirely phantasmal. An old Shaker spiritual reminds us that just as surely as "'Tis a gift to be free," it is also "a gift to be *simple*," simplicity reflecting the twin mysteries of Nature's comprehensibility and its describability (e.g., in poetry and differential equations). It and we must somehow be of a piece—different, yet clearly cut from the same whole cloth.)

(Stage directions continued: Sketch a pipe on blackboard. Wave a "real" pipe before awed students.) *This* (point with pipe to exquisite sketch on chalkboard) is *not* a pipe (Magritte cited by Foucault 1983). My word, *pipe*, is *not* a pipe. *Here* (wave pipe once more) is a pipe, whatever that "really" is.

In the realm of language there are no absolutes, only a democracy of possibilities. You can call this (nimbly juggle fruit) "orange" or you can call it "Bart." Describe the sky as "blue" or "X." These names have equal absolute meaning: none. There is no authority among words, all of which are equals.

But such equality does not exist in the realm of the thing itself, which, however briefly, *is*. For example, that which we identify as the sky is a chimera, i.e., not exactly what it seems to be. Like all mirages, however, the sky signifies in a way that its purely abstract name does not. In this case, the sky represents—no, it *is*—the handiwork of a dynamic alliance of solar energy and atmosphere.

The orange, my pipe, the lectern, an aurora, the sky: none is clearly, simplistically objective, but each is ineluctably, profanely, unlike the perfect subjectivity of the mere idea. There is a difference between arbitrary name and immanent nature—a fuzzy difference sometimes, but one which we ignore at our peril, especially in the realm of the great regularities, like gravity, death, and so forth.

To put it simplistically, I worry that too many people of the 1990s have adopted not only a worldview of "anything goes" but have (almost) convinced themselves that anything can "go" at no cost. They have confused the subjective, absolute-less democracy of language with the objective Truth of reality. If, for example, it is a lovely and profound postmodern metaphor to say that every human—every *thing*, even—is as "beautiful" as every other, it is also literally true that *some* cells are cancer cells and that *some* humans are serial killers. Who shall inform a cancer of its "inauthenticity"? If you weigh 400 pounds, is your personal worth in the subjective realm equal to that of someone who weighs 150 pounds?  Of course; without question.  Do not, however, be seduced into the belief that such equality applies to the objective realm of Nature.  Put only partly metaphorically, the universe punishes those who defy it.  All else being equal, the fat die before the thin.  To deny this is to accede to the proposition that your child (or your neighbor) is naught but an undigested bit of protein, and, finally, that you are likewise.

I think not.  Whether you are essentially walking dirt, thinking vortex, cosmic consciousness, or speaking spirit, I cannot say, but in some manner you *are*, of that I am confident.  Unless one is willing to deny the significance—not necessarily the primacy, but at least some meaning—of existence, the Real (however temporary and elusive) has an authority which the simulated and the purely symbolic lack.  To deny this seems no problem for solipsists and other magicians (a curious facility, considering their existential roots) but is counterintuitive for the rest of us.

You have come of age in an age not of the reality of virtue nor of the virtue of reality but of "virtual reality."  The proxy world of video games is but a step in the direction of the high-tech virtual systems which will shortly be a living-room reality, at which point one will acquire pleasure without the messy actualities of people and planet.  Although this is in principle an age of the transcendence of *experience* (rather than that of the divine, the ideal, or any form of Other), it is in fact a time of passivity, of simulation, and of mediation.  For every expert athlete who has single-mindedly striven in pursuit of mastery, there are hundreds of thousands of armchair devotees.  For every serious reader there are millions of functional "literates" to whom Huck Finn, Ahab, Scrooge and Wordsworth's "Daffodils" have never spoken a single syllable.  For every creator like Matt Groening, there are uncountable ranks of Bart Simpsons.

You are yet young, and so are forgiven—temporarily!—your bedazzlement with kitsch.  Wallyworld or South Padre Island—any foray into the sphere of the frivolous, the false, even—is a harmless enough spring-break diversion.  For us old geezers, however, there are no excuses.  There comes a time when one must discriminate between the genuine and the counterfeit.  Anyone over forty who suggests to you that there is no difference between being and nonbeing has never experienced Experience and is thus in grave danger of committing the unforgivable sin: dying without having lived.

Moments of truth occur on the intellectual as well as on the spiritual path.  One of the most important of all such epiphanies begins with the awful realization that the ideal one has been seeking (whether the divine ideal or the ideal of truth) is a product of one's own sense-impressions and imagination and is therefore fundamentally limited, probably even "wrong."  If the image is flawed, one tends to conclude, the ideal itself must be false.  That which *I* cannot experience (divinity) or know (truth) cannot be.

Beware the indulgence of this arrogance. The Real was here for quite some time before you showed up. After you are gone, I expect that it will continue somehow to carry on. Don't take yourself so seriously. More to the point, remember that you have reached this pinnacle of illumination only because of your ideal. It carried you here. There are no other vehicles to these aeries. You know that you know very little only because, finally, you know quite a lot, knowledge gained through your devotion to and pursuit of your ideal. However, your ascent thus far has merely brought you to a plateau. Beyond, above, lies the numinous. To go higher, your imagination must expand, carrying as it does your ideal a bit closer to the Real.

The stream of Nature's tao *is*. Indeed, "in the beginning was rhythm, and rhythm was made flesh" (Cendrars 1970). One need only to go to the beach to verify this. Sit quietly. Experience the sloshing waves, the ruffling breeze, the wheeling gulls, the squalling infants, your own heartbeat. Yes, there is an undeniable Memorex-like quality of falseness to one's *experience* of the field of being. That's the downside of consciousness. And yet, notwithstanding the self-limiting nature of sense perceptions, you *are* a part of that which is True.

Weather consists of the totality of an unending parade of gyres, from leaf-whirls to hurricanes, each of which is both a "self"—so to speak—and also a minor player in the collectivity of atmospheric circulation. Although each vortex is temporary and linked to the larger system, *there is no atmospheric circulation without them*. So, too, the full significance of any particular thing, or life, rests neither just on itself phenomenally nor only on the ceaseless, thingless, noumenal flow of fluxes but on the relationship of the two.

Yours will be the first truly postmodern generation. The first century of the third millennium, your century, will witness the coming of age of a fourth worldview. It could be that of the solipsism of the "narcissistic conformist" (Heller 1990). I hope not, for in that maze lies the most pitiless of all prisons, that of isolation. Whereas solitude finds one alone with the Absolute, in isolation one is absolutely alone with oneself. When loneliness is merely a part of the inwardness of the isolated individual, it consumes and diminishes (Picard 1952); for the sense that only the self is real is but a step away from the belief that *nothing* is real. Roger Scruton summarized the antilogic of political solipsism thus: "At some point, the person who asks 'why should I do that?' of every custom and every law, must force upon himself the more devastating question, 'why should I do anything?'" (1980). A note of despair has crept into the voice of even so hopeful an observer as Jacques Barzun:

> [The] quality of life was partly recovered during the period between wars but was utterly lost again. My present sense of surroundings is thus akin to that of my childhood in wartime. Crime on the streets, hijacking in the air, hostage-taking and

bombing in once well-policed countries—this state of seige, coupled with the daily warnings of danger from food and drink, medication and machinery, clothing, toys, and sex, viruses and killer diseases seconded by polluted air and water, has reconstituted the situation of permanent *qui vive*. Even when no thought of nuclear war is present to the mind, the atmosphere forbids delectation, let alone complacency. (1990)

Long, long ago, as Saint Augustine observed the end of his age from his deathbed, Roman certainties crashing down while the Vandal hordes overran Hippo, his fusion of New Testament and Platonic traditions gave him hope that an even better order would follow. A thousand years later, more or less, Thomas Aquinas, unifying Aristotelian reason with Christian transcendency, spoke of humankind's position at the conjunction of the corporeal and the spiritual, voicing a metaphysical equivalent of the Archimedian "Eureka!"

Your challenge (not terribly much greater than those of Augustine and Aquinas combined, I trust) is the realization of a *syncretic* worldview, a complementary reconciliation of antinomies, different, true images of Nature: of the broken symmetries of countless particular, accidental, ephemeral fluxes, whirling together and comprising a ceaseless, streamlike flow, whose deepest, most familiar pulselike cadences are irreducibly, sublimely simple. Essential. True. Tao.

Like all such transitions, yours will be what the Chinese wryly call an "interesting" time. Often terrible, but—for the brave, humble, and grateful of heart—more often terrific. And so I close by urging you, as Jacques Barzun puts it, to "fight the mechanical" (1990), and to always remember that you are a pilgrim.

## Note

1. "Why," one may ask, "did the religious worldview emerge victorious?" "Wishful thinking," we intellectuals often reply. Perhaps. Perhaps not. Why does rock music retain such popular favor in the same West that produced classic masterpieces of reasoned perfection? If you reply, peeved at the obviousness of the answer, "These simple, elementary rhythms and melodies appeal to the ignorant masses!" I suggest that you have overlooked the allure these tunes have for many of our best and brightest, the future Einsteins, Kierkegaards and, yes, Mozarts. The symphonies of Beethoven and the most complicated machines, Blaise Cendrars has written, move according to identical laws: they progress arithmetically, and they are ruled by a need for symmetry which breaks down their motion into a series of minuscule and identical measures (1970).

In contrast, the Faust-like charm of much rock music lies precisely in its animality: it *is* fundamentally simple; the cerebral is the surest path to altering Nature, perhaps even to understanding it, but not to participating in its dance. "In the beginning was rhythm, and rhythm was made flesh" (ibid.). When people harken to the primordial beat of rock music, they almost universally intuit their originary carnal connections with the Other. How do art and, particularly, music permit such an encounter? This is like asking how the mind can comprehend the nature of things. One cannot be sure that the answer is "Because such internal patterns in some way mirror external ones," but that answer seems at least as plausible as "dumb luck."

## Review and Reflections on the Text

1. Define noumenal; noosphere; numinous.

2. What is the relationship of "true teachers" to ignorance?

3. Examine the logic underlying the author's assertion that "True teachers much also be true believers." What does he mean, and what is the necessary connection between teaching and faith? Discuss these questions in small groups or as a class.

4. G. K. Chesterton found scientific explanations of natural phenomena unsatisfying. Do you? Why or why not?

5. Explain in your own words the distinction the author makes between "true knowledge" and *Truth*. Choose a familiar object and try to describe it in the neutral, objective terms of "true knowledge." In what respects is this description inadequate, incomplete, or even false?

6. What does the author mean to suggest with his image of a stream vortex that is aware of all other currents to which it is even indirectly connected? What does this image have to do with sustaining a sense of wonder?

7. In what sense is the emerging worldview reflected in the metaphoric disappearance of Nature from postmodern consciousness? (What does the author mean when he refers to capital-N "Nature," anyway?) Why is the notion that Nature has *literally* disappeared a "grievous error"?

8. What does the concept of honor mean to you? Discuss this question with friends or classmates to see if you can find points of consensus on what honor is and whether it has value.

9.    The author quotes Jacques Barzun as asserting that the right of Equality is "the right to every other right" and that "Equality implies Reciprocity." Respond in writing to these ideas.  How would they apply to situations and decisions in your own life?

10.    The author suggests that postexistential denials of the possibility of Truth are superstitious "magic" and speaks of "the magic of a self-love."  What is the term *magic* meant to convey?

11.    What are "magic circles"?  Why are they dangerous?  Can you think of anything good to say about them?

12.    Do you agree with the author that the arbitrariness of language does not exist in the realm of things-in-themselves?  Can language, arbitrary as it is, affect things-in-themselves?  Explain your answer.

13.    In what sense does "the Real" have more *authority* than the symbolic and the simulated?    (For instance, how does looking at the Grand Canyon compare with looking at pictures of the Grand Canyon?)

14.    How is weather like a basketball team?  An acting company?  A class? A community?  How is it unlike them?

15.    What is the difference between solitude and isolation?

16.    What do you think is (or will be) the "fourth paradigm"?    Write a paragraph explaining or describing what the fourth paradigm is.  Write one explaining or describing your own current worldview.    Compare your reflections with those of others and discuss them together.

# VII. Lost In Cyberland: The Last Texians

Every quality which leads to eminence in human history represents, on one side of it, an extension of a force of nature by which the harmonies of nature are disturbed, the inequalities of nature accentuated, the cruelties of nature aggravated and human history involved in self-destruction. These tragic aspects of human excellence and superiority are usually obscured in history. They become fully apparent only in rare moments when empires and civilisations decay and when it is recognized that they were brought low, not by some external foe but by the defect of their own virtues.

—Reinhold Niebuhr, *Beyond Tragedy*

All, all dead, and ourselves left alone amidst a new generation whom we know not, and who knows not us.

—Thomas Jefferson, c.1825

"Holy Toledo."

Having just returned to South Texas from a brief fin-de-semester holiday, digesting a week's worth of headlines, I was muttering imprecations in the general direction of my wife. A veteran university groundskeeper working alongside a street on the edge of the campus had been run down and killed by a hit-and-run driver. In a nearby hamlet visited by a scourge of absolutely conscienceless juvenile criminals, four hundred citizens, some toting shotguns, publicly threatened to "take matters into their own hands." Two elderly women—one a close friend—had been molested and robbed in their homes. . .

"Holy Moly."

Several more area churches had been torched (one youthful arsonist explaining that he "was bored"). A gentle seventy-four-year-old recluse murdered at home for, as it turned out, his driver's license and library card. An accelerating pandemic of irrational urban homicides (such as drive-by shootings done for no other reason than meanness), this in a state where the

93

.the average time behind bars for murder is two years, and where the total number of prisoners already is exceeded only in places like California and South Africa. . .

"Holy Cow!"

"Honey, please." With a weary smile, Lottie peered at me through a declivity in the cordillera of bills and junk mail which she was sorting. "You sound like Harry Carry when the Cubs muff an easy grounder: 'It wasn't like this in the Good Old Days!' Calm down."

"Sorry," I replied, gazing half-consciously at a pair of sparrows who (ignoring my various repellant schemes) were putting the finishing touches on a nest tucked securely under the eaves of our patio. But maybe, I mused, just maybe this time Harry's right. I thought of a conversation which, although it felt as though it might have occurred the day before yesterday, was in fact almost exactly twenty years old, at the time of our first visit to subtropical Texas. Having left Chicago blanketed in eight humorless inches of equinoctial snow, Lottie and I were more than ready to be assured, as we were by a senior faculty member, that "although you may not get rich here, because of our traditional values you'll never have to lock your doors or worry about being raped." What's happened?

Maybe nothing. Perhaps, I comfort myself, not only was the old professor guilty of extravagant naiveté but the experience of old fogies like me is inevitably—virtually by definition—that of unravelling places and devolving times. Maybe it was never safe to leave our doors unlocked, for our values and behavior have *really* always been about as they are now.

Not.

Last week, walking from home to administer a final examination, I passed a crowd gathered around a student who'd been run down in a campus crosswalk. My teeth gnashed involuntarily. Another one! Later, while distributing the exam papers, I bleated at my students to "be careful" and "consider how awful it would be to kill someone." Their replies: "Hey, it was raining." "I heard she ran across the street without looking." "Yeah, and the umbrella blocked her vision." "The poor guy tried to stop, but skidded on the wet pavement." No mention of the university speed limit of 20 MPH (which even the campus cops exceed) nor of crosswalks as sacrosanct, much less the irreplaceable human singularity of the victim herself (who, fortunately, was only severely bruised). I shook my head in dismay. Texians[1] have always driven like banshees, with excess hubris, and often foolishly (e.g., packing loaded deer rifles and loaded coolers), but not solipsistically. In fact, a working definition of "Texian" might once have been, "Would prefer to shoot himself than live with the memory of killing a bike-riding kid."

No longer. Houston freeways have of course become the stuff of legend—where else will dozens of cars mash a pedestrian into unrecognizable goo?—but even our rural highways are mean Brownian frenzies. Driving at the speed limit is as hazardous on State Highway 77 between Corpus Christi and Brownsville as it is on Interstate 35 between Austin and Dallas. Driving in Texas now is much like visiting a friend in a maximum-security asylum for psychopaths: you do it, but nervously.

After the last student submitted with a sigh her exam paper, I escaped to a rare subtropical spring day. The reverie of my stroll was, however, soon interruped by an aerial admonishment to "Have a delicious Coca-Cola!" which was crawling across the largest free-standing sign on campus, donated several years ago by guess-who. "Good Lord!" I thought (or exclaimed, I suppose, judging by the glares of several passers-by). "'Don't worry, be happy. Shit happens. Veni, vidi, Visa.' I've been worrying about killer bees and missed the real invasion: kitsch."

That night, still brooding, I complained, "Who *are* these jerks? They can't all be expatriate New Yorkers. What happened to the Texians? Where did they go? Alaska?"

Lottie shook her head, smiling. This was familiar territory. "Don't be silly. There are Texans  'Texians' if you insist—all around you."

"Oh, no. Broke, wannabe Californians, maybe, but definitely *not* Texians. Wherever he is, Protagoras[2] must be feeling pretty smug.

"What about me?" she countered.

"You're an anachronism. A living fossil. The last Texian. The rest are dead and gone now, but *I* remember them. I remember the other Lotties..."

The sentence drifted, incomplete, as my thoughts wandered back to the East Texas to which we had moved in the mid-sixties so that Lottie could regraft herself onto Lufkin rootstock. "Deep East Texas" was for me a revelation, a new world as exotic as Tibet. My wife's aging kinfolks—and many others then still extant—were usually larger than life, occasionally grotesque, invariably genuine. Dickens would have recognized them in a heartbeat. Theirs were the memories of unmediated experience: stories of limbless civil war vets, of grinding hardship, of overgrown acres of toddlers killed by the flu and spouses by overwork, of the happiness which transcends mere pleasure. The satisfaction of a life lived elementally. Authentically. Death was hard, mostly, and always uncompromising, but most Texians were believers of one sort or another, and part of their faith demanded a mighty struggle against the final embrace of that good night.

And daily discourse, well, that alone was worth the not inconsiderable psychic cost of a Texas visa. Back in the Corn Belt we spoke the finest plain-vanilla American English. Oh, sometimes we Calvinists did speak a kind of minimalist prose, perhaps even haiku. Notwithstanding our near-Confucian work ethic (and our consequently good material lives), though, meaning for us lay, finally, not in the trials of profane daily life but elsewhere, in Other. The Texian tongue, however—here was a collage of allegory and image whose significance derived more from contingent but concrete existence than from transcendent verities. Memorable throw-away lines, themselves extracted from lives lived between rocks and hard places, rolled by like limbs on a risen creek. The language of these people of the word, as unselfconscious as August cockroaches, was one which illuminated the essential through a celebration of those ephemeral moving images of eternity, as Plato called daily lives.

If Texians were diamondlike prisms to real presences, they had also the sharp edges of rough gems. You could be eaten by the earth in these parts, and they marshaled their defenses accordingly. Under very limited but not uncommon circumstances, these folks'd shoot you and bury your body in a cottonwood grove or feed you to the stock. Nightmarish stuff, forever inexcusable this side of Perfection.

Could any world be worse, you ask, than one which works for insiders but excludes those on its margins? Of course: one which is unsuccessful all the way through. Texas had a gritty but dependable internal integrity. What you saw *was*, by and large, what you got. If you were broken down alongside the road, they'd stop to help, irrespective of class or race. But more to the point, the primary test of any worldview is I think whether it contributes to the ongoing human quest for such ultimate ends as identity, harmony, and understanding. Texians could certainly be hypocrites (the practice of universal Christian brotherhood—much less sisterhood—was often a characteristic shortcoming), but because they could feel shame they not uncommonly developed wisdom. Their approach to life often did not accommodate outsiders, especially the marginalized, but *for them* it passed the primary *Weltanschauung* test: it worked.

A month ago, my students participated in a "values survey" of several thousand Texas undergraduates. One of the first statements to which they were asked to respond was the following: "My opinion is as valid as that of a more knowledgeable person." One of the last was that "every idea has equal worth." The students overwhelmingly agreed (usually "strongly") with both statements. As recently as a generation ago most Texians—however formally uneducated—would I think have scoffed at the solipsism of such kitsch-think, recognizing (to paraphrase Plato and Heidegger) that just as being requires boundaries, so too does freedom. Distinctions exist (e.g., some things are real, others are not) as do hierarchies—some ideas are better than others (the heliocentric rather than geocentric solar system, say, or the notion of the equal worth of individual humans compared with the notion of Aryan superiority).

The ultimate metaphysical power of difference is undeniable: If Perfection be so perfect, why a universe of particularities? Nevertheless, differentness is not *always* preferable to sameness. Difference and change may be either good or bad. (Compare, for instance, New York City's livability circa 1950 and today. Or consider the recent increased "diversity" in southern Texas due to the invasions of fire ants and Africanized bees, which to date seem to offer no discernible good end. . .) The presumed advantages of difference are particularly questionable when perceived difference is merely a mask for sameness. For all our talk of diversity, ersatz Texas increasingly seems to me a place of ever-flatter mindscapes, where noise has shamelessly driven silence into hiding, where potent metaphorical Truth ("You're only as old as you feel," etc.) is drained of all meaning by trivialization into literal "true knowledge"; where, in other words, anything and everything is tolerated *except* true differentness. (Although most of the great contributors to the intellectual adventure, as well as the spiritual quest, have almost by definition been idiosyncratic oddballs, try to find a Mr. Chips or any "character" teaching today in a Texas public school.)

This veneer of difference is Kundera's kitsch, the brotherhood of the false. Love was, for instance, once understood to be a kind of real presence, perhaps the only one able somehow to come across the horizon from Other itself. Like the Hebrew God, Yahweh, it was too precious for prattle. Now, in ersatz Texas, we blather endlessly about that in which we no longer believe, having lost faith not only in love but in all such Kantian presences: goodness, beauty, truth. Hence, I suppose, our denial of the tragedy, the fundamental imperfectability, of life and all of existence, in favor of magical utopianism: all problems are either illusions or are soluble. Any day I expect to be assured that, really, the gates to Paradise are wide and greased (paradise being, of course, merely one more real absence).

Baloney. Even if we eventually manage to allay suffering and transmute death (probably consciousnesses downloaded into computer-robots, yum), knowledge itself is by definition a finite or imperfect proxy of whatever Truth is. Truth in this ultimate sense may well lie beyond the bounds of time and space, but *here* is where ice cream and bluebonnets, kisses and ideas are to be found. Even our relationship to the tangible "stuff" for which we are infamous—cars and Air Jordans and sex, for that matter—seems one of compulsive diversion, like mindlessly eating handful after handful of potato chips, than an experience of the merely real or merely beautiful (as likely as anything else to represent the "meaning" of existence), which have become sufficiently foreign to normal daily life that they can appear exotic or at least eccentric.

(A small personal aside: In beginning science classes the most essential requisite after curiosity is observation. To be worthwhile, observation demands devoted, focused concentration on something in particular, but contemporary American undergraduates are conditioned to experiencing the world, especially the nonhuman world, in relatively passive, mediated ways (e.g., TV, spectator sports, mall atriums). Environment as Musak. As a precursor to actual observation, I have found it useful to take my students outdoors occasionally on directed rambles, during which they are asked to notice things more carefully than usual. Pretty effective, sometimes. Try, however, explaining a walking meditation on a standardized Annual Faculty Performance Review form, documents close in spirit to IRS or Postal Service products.)

My wife and I recently spent several days at a pleasant old hotel on the absolute edge of the known universe in Bayside, a Copano Bay village of countless memories and 381 living residents. The only guests, we rattled about among twenty bedrooms, two porches, formal parlors upstairs and down, dining room, library and gameroom. Everywhere we were haunted by ghosts of conversations and of silences. Why else retreat to the shore but to plunge into the hermitage of silence *and* the collectivity of conversation? One of the most painful ironies of postmodernity is that noise has dispatched both silence *and* conversation, to the extent that each is becoming ever more dimly recollected. At least once each week, even toward the close of a semester, I must beg my students to please, for God's sake, be quiet! They of course intend no disrespect. Noise, including babble (the kitsch counterpart to conversation) has become for them  *autonomic*, as unselfconscious as breathing. I exaggerate, you say? Listen to what passes for conversation among "Texans"—intelligent, educated ones, even—under age, oh, 35 or so (assuming that you can even *hear* them over the din of street clatter, background "music" and the ceaseless general din which is the canticle of the postmodern good life. . .).

Western worldviews, reacting against classical realism, have been riding a rising rationalist tide ever since Descartes. Mind over matter. Thus, we have come to presume not merely that everything's made out of ideas (Platonic idealism), nor even that things have no existence apart from perception of them (Berkeley's subjective idealism)—both of which retain a place for Other—but that *our* perception of anything is essential for it to be.

As knowledge, mind, and mood ascended to primacy, as all realities became social and psychological creations, the old objective truth of Being became as embarrassing a chimera as Santa Claus or phlogiston. Now Texans—once "forces of nature" themselves—and Texas—the last American redoubt of realism, product equally of high culture and low, where authenticity was always central—have become as deconstructed as Detroit.

Even a change which proves eventually to be on balance "good" may not be so immediately. Saint Augustine's trust that the Roman world crashing about him in Hippo would be replaced by something even better was finally vindicated, but only after a long and—for many—nasty age of transition. Texas is entering such a transition now, a generation after most of the rest of the Western world. With any luck it will be followed in a half-century or so by a new and harmonious marriage of the children of tradition (community) and modernity (individualism). For now, however, these postmodern adolescents are nightmarish admixtures of the worst of their lineages: tribal conformity (e.g., machismo) on the one hand, and the narcissistic conformity of solipsism on the other.

Twenty-five years ago, Eric Hoffer described twentieth-century culture as something made by "juvenile delinquents." Doubtless Hoffer had in mind the ongoing trivialization of our interests and the concomitant kitschification of more and more of the stuff of our culture. (Recall, for instance, the recent interdenominational quarrel among equally true believers on the weighty matter of the Presley postage stamp: should Elvis's visage be of the rude but innocent Prince or of the corpulent, world-weary King?) Today, in a fin-de-millennium Texas where the only assumed certainty is that anything goes, the end of the Time of Juveniles remains nowhere in sight.

As I write, my wife is back in East Texas for the burial of the aunt after whom she was named. Soon they'll all be gone, these artifact Lotties, as distant in memory as the Pharoahs. Not forgotten, precisely, but worse: dismissed as fictitious, so many simple-minded, not-quite-digested bits of fable and dream. We masters of revisionism, paralyzed within our enchanted circles of kitsch, as historically befuddled as Reagan, will soon have ourselves convinced that there never were any Texians, really. John Wayne, the Alamo, Texas itself: all equally mythic, and less, merely tall tales.

But not quite yet. Not so long as a few of us linger who recall those *monstres sacres*, the Lotties and their kind.

The last Texians.

## Notes

1. "Texian," a term popularized by Mirabeau B. Lamar to encourage national character, was widely used in colonial and revolutionary Texas (about 1821-1845) and sporadically thereafter. Probably intended only for citizens of the Republic of northern European stock, it was—happily—soon adopted by others as well.

2. Protagoras, a contemporary of Socrates, asserted that "man is the measure of all things."

## Review and Reflections on the Text

1.   Review the author's comments about Texians.  How would you explain, in your own words, what Texians are?

2.   What are the implied connections among the spread of kitsch, the ascendance of rational over realist worldviews, and the disappearance of the Texians?

3.   Explain why observation, to be worthwhile, must be an active process.

4.   What does the author mean when he says that "noise has dispatched both silence *and* conversation"?

5.   What is the nature of the transition the author describes as taking place in Texas?  What are its current symptoms?  What does the author view as a desirable outcome?  What do you view as a probable outcome?

# Postface

There is no logical reason for the existence of a snowflake any more than
there is for evolution. It is an apparition from that mysterious shadow world
beyond nature, that final world which contains—if anything contains—the
explanation of men and catfish and green leaves.

Loren Elseley, *The Immense Journey*

Contemporary philosophers suggest that whereas the traditional "fear of
death" was that of never connecting with the Ultimate, its postmodern
equivalent is that of never breaking free to forge one's own identity.
According to the former, at least ideally one aspired to submerge or even to
annihilate self, in the latter, any Ultimate being presumed either nonsensical
or forever inaccessible, valor and virtue lie in the creation of that which is
distinctively Me.

Is this as egocentric as it sounds? In principle, no. The modern
undercurrent which gathered strength over several centuries, right up to
almost the day before yesterday, that I (and, often, only I) am sacred, now
feels as vanquished, as absolutely irretrievable, as Ozimandias' kingdom. The
self, like everything else, is now seen as absolutely contingent or unnecessary.
Pursuing meaning (so to speak) via this postmodern tao is thus a very brave
undertaking, for it requires making what we will of our own "texts," becoming
"strong poets" who celebrate ourselves as happenstance children of chance
and time. To profess in the midst of a trek through Cyberland—where by
definition reality is a contemporary inside joke, like "a politician's honor" or
"Cleveland's scenic wonders"—that "I am the only reality" sounds like a line
from Lewis Carroll or Monty Python. Hubris on the surface but in fact so
chastened as to hint at a willingness to venture beyond solipsism or (returning
to the remark of Andrei Codrescu which set us off on this little journey) to
give up the ideal for the real. Pretty impressive, and hopeful, stuff.

On the other hand, the actual postmodernish *practice* of ordinary
people in their day-to-day lives has often become more that of anything goes,

the perverted shadow of the postmodernist's "anything *may* go." Popular culture, shot through, informed, and often driven by the legacies of tradition and classicism for countless generations, has recently gone more than a little insane. Intuiting a future bereft of the old certainties, we opted for the magic of solipsistic romanticism: *my* will be done. As a consequence, although at some instinctive level we recognize that we have escaped into a cul-de-sac, egomaniacal behavior and attitudes have in these closing years of the second millennium become so assumed, so thoroughly normal—*I* must be happy, *I* am as intelligent as Einstein, *I'll* decide the speed at which I drive (and so on; see Chapters V-VII)—as to be our last redoubt of "true."

What to make of this? About the postmodern split with sacredness I can tell you nothing. It is true that I think that there are real presences, that these are what we seek via the taos we discover/create, and that we are farther along in that quest than we have ever been, but I can't demonstrate or even logically defend any of those notions, other than to remind you of my earlier anecdote about fishing in murky waters.

Concerning the postmodernish loss of faith in meaning, however, I implore you to recognize it as a temporary but dangerous abberration. Thirty years ago being a jerk was, up to a point, an appropriate act of social rebellion, something akin to a Taoist response to narrow Confucian strictures. Today, to resist the increasing cyberpunkification of our behavior and outlook is to be subversive in the best sense of the word. To paraphrase Yevgeny Yevtushenko, there is only one avenue to true happiness. It is that of a devoted pilgrim making her way toward meaning via the benchmarks of Other. Perhaps we should say "Others": the things of Nature; people and the entire humanified world; ideas; and the realm of the holy, whatever that may be. (Doubtless a very redundant listing.) It is quite true that the pilgrim is lost much of the time and that being lost is uncomfortable. Sorry. Do you want understanding or comfort? You can't have it all.

Cultivate the knack of simplicity. It is easy to collapse under the immense postmodernish weight of infinite detail and uncountable choices, all supposedly equally important and valid. An old Christian prayer begs, "Teach me to care, and not to care." Care for that which enables oneself and others to break free of the chains of ignorance and to pursue paths of meaning, and not care about the rest.

The useful is no more and no less than that, a utilitarian means of transportation in the direction of an ideal. Identity or community, for example. All paths to ideal states, however, pass through the real. Value the true. There is no other way.

*Memento mori.* (Remember, you must die.) Get moving!

Vaya con Dios.

# Appendix:
# Wanderings

[On returning home from another society] a strange alienness grips you, not because anything has changed but rather because you no longer see things as "natural" or "normal." . . . You find yourself discussing the things that seem important to your friends with the same detached seriousness that you used to discuss witchcraft with your villagers. Anything connected with shopping seems inordinately difficult. . . . Polite conversation is extraordinarily hard. Long silences are taken as brooding displeasure while people in the street react quite badly to the sight of a man quite openly talking to himself. . . .

—Nigel Barley, *The Innocent Anthropologist*

## 1. Egypt—July 1990

### El Alamein

Alexandria looks something like Acapulco—same gorgeous curving bay, same out-of-town refugees—but is far older, seedier, and more arresting. People on the streets are considerably more Western than in Cairo, much less the rest of Egypt. Many women, perhaps one-third, wear no head-covering at all. Adolescents wear the universal uniform of jeans, t-shirt and sneakers. There are joggers, even a few in shorts. Still, Alexandria is much more "traditional" a place than Acapulco. If, to date, modernity remains the icing on a solidly Arab Islamic cake, Acapulco's look and, even more, its outlook, have been transformed into something fast approaching *post*modern. A lobster fajita, perhaps. The salsa, however authentic, is the veneer.

However, Alexandria itself may be collapsing under the weight of that modern icing, overwhelmed and sinking under sheer numbers. The bay stinks of sewerage yet fisherman line the cornice. Litter is everywhere. The streets are shifting scenes of human gridlock, noise, and hazard. The constant assault on the senses is acute and wearing.

What all this means is unclear. Yesterday, over tea-shop *shai* and pipes—my meershaum and his water-bubbler—I chatted with a young Alexandria University student. Comparing notes on the unfolding World Cup in his limited English and my nearly nonexistent Arabic, we agreed that the two luckiest teams seemed to be bumbling toward the finals. (We were only half right: England lost in the semi-finals.) Seemingly thoroughly modern, my friend became genuinely engaged only when I confessed my interest in Sufism, Islamic mysticism.

"Oh yes. My mind is modern, you see," he told me, "but my heart is Islamic."

This morning I asked two accompanying Egyptologists why the locals so incessantly honk their car horns ("incessant" meaning with such professional style, perseverance and sheer volume as to relegate Delhi and Mexico City to the furthermost minor leagues).

One replied, "I don't know." How has he gotten so far in academe? I wondered, admiringly.

The other expert, however, offered a brilliantly priggish rationale, the gist of which was that Egyptian traffic offers such an unpredictable yet constant all-out assault that, batlike, drivers must "fix" one another via ceaseless honking. In other words, the reason for the craziness of Egyptian hornplay is the craziness of Egyptian driving. . . Such inspired circular reasoning is the stuff of endowed chairs.

In late morning we arrive at the British and German World War II monuments at El Alamein, on the Mediterranean coast west of Alexandria. The massive German memorial is impersonal, stolidly monumental. It appears to commemorate a principle, an abstraction, rather than actual people. The British graveyard is different. Eight thousand Commonwealth soldiers who died in the campaigns of 1940-1943 are interred here.

I wander among the spare white markers. The ground is quite bare, all brown sands, except for a brave scattering of flowering trees and shrubs. Idly, I begin to read inscriptions. Many echo of a hollow vainglory. "No greater love," "Not forgotten," "Not in vain," "A British soldier's noble end," and the like. I have no quarrel with the sincerity of intent but, ultimately, they miss the point. Like all of us, these will be forgotten. Questions of victory or defeat are strictly for the living.

Other inscriptions are less grand, almost humdrum. They bring to mind images of doughty, fortyish parents in Saffron Waldren; of pallid wives in Glasgow; of children never known in Christchurch. Yvonne Pamela Denton writes to her forever 26-year-old husband, Lt. D. Denton, "When we were young." On the marker of J. Chalmers, 23-year-old member of the Black

Watch, is written: "We will meet again some-day, son.  Maw, Paw, Lena & Davy."

I am shocked to find unbidden tears coursing my cheeks, as they shall continue to do for the next half-hour.

Phrases like "Treasured memories of our darling daddy," "Dear son in the daylight / whom in the darkness we won't forget," "To have him in the same old way / would be our greatest wish today," and "Gone is the light from these blue eyes"—sentimental, silly really—are, because of their irreducible humanness, shattering.  No vainglory this, merely extraordinary ordinariness.

Coming from my postmodern world of angst and anomie, being plunged back into the realm of the genuine is more than I can bear.  Stupidly, I snap at a colleague who quite innocently aproaches to blather about matters of fact.  Plucking a blossom from an acacia tree, I turn to stare south into the great Sahara.  Perfectly inaccessible, it only magnifies my grief.  These foolish, soon-to-be-forgotten little bits of walking dirt, now eaten by the earth, were the stuff of meaning, for if there is any "purpose" to existence, it is to be found in such "productions of time," to paraphrase Blake.  What is victory compared with knowledge?  What is knowledge beside a daffodil or, better, a kiss?  "When we were young. . ."

As we are leaving, a half-dozen ragamuffins gather to beg, "Baksheesh, baksheesh!"  Exactly the dirty, greedy urchins for which I long.  I dispense candies, apples and Little Debbie snack cakes, whispering, "You little magpies" (they don't know a word of English), meaning, I suppose, "Thanks."

Back on the bus, our local scholar-guide immediately launches into a prolonged, P.A.-enhanced historical monologue, a treasure-trove of facts about the El Alamein battles.  As exercise in computerlike recall, it is an impressive demonstration.  Nothing wrong with information, but just now it is beside the point.  Alas, we poor professors, I muse bitterly.  Intelligence so near, wisdom so remote.

Just up the desert highway lies Wadi Natron, the desert valley or "oasis" in which are several ancient Coptic Christian monasteries. Monastacism is one of Egypt's greatest and least appreciated contributions to world civilization.  Although there were by the fifth century several hundred monasteries in Wadi Natron, only four survive.

Passing from the desert landscape through the monastery's thick walls into an inner courtyard, one immediately experiences a sense of retreat, even solitude, notwithstanding the four busloads of tourists.

Inside, standing before the millennium-old carved sanctuary door, a bearded young monk named Father Johannus spoke of the monastery's history and purpose.  He tells us of Saint Bishoy, who was perhaps the prototype for the Saint Christopher legend and who remains a particular Coptic favorite. (It is said that he once passed up an opportunity to meet Christ in order to assist an old man who turned out to be the Savior.)  Father "John's" gentle presence speaks volumes. If, as it is said, all true mystics reveal themselves in serenity of speech and expression, this good monk qualifies.

Just south of Wadi Natron lies Sadat City, one of three "satellite cities" being developed by the Egyptian government about sixty miles from Cairo. "Sadat City" to date remains a misnomer, for only 2,000 residents occupy a facility designed for 50,000.

Between Sadat City and Cairo, the Desert Highway penetrates the margin of the Sahara. Still, along this entire stretch private dairy farms, citrus orchards, arbors and other agricultural enterprises are springing into existence. In this incredibly arid setting—average yearly rainfall is less than one inch—these farms will surely blow away if, or more likely when, their wells fail. The Sahara, like all predators, has teeth.

In late afternoon, the Pyramids of Giza appear ahead through a pastiche of power lines, concrete plants and billboards.

"Hurray!" we novices cheer.

Half-turning, our porta-pedant interrupts his latest monologue just long enough to inform us that we can "come out to these pyramid-shaped structures later in the week" on our own time. Not even a photo op. We stare incredulously at one other.

Gazing a temporary farewell, I note that the Pyramids will soon be thoroughly encircled by residential "Nasser City" and similar Lilliputians. Catching a final glimpse of these glorious, captive behemoths, realizing that the dinosaurs may have been luckier than I'd ever considered, I experience a moment of perverse gratitude that I won't be around to visit the ruins of postmodern Cairo in, say, 2050. The still-evolving, or -devolving, *modern* incarnation—Cairo 1990—to which we now return is quite enough for this aging misanthrope.

### Sikkara

Zozer's Stepped Pyramid at Sikkara (c.2650 B.C.) sits hermetically, aloofly alone in the desert, just beyond Cairo's reach. This is how Giza must have been, should be. Remote enough to register, properly, as alien.

Still, if art is a lie which teaches the truth, as Picasso maintained, no pyramid is art. What fiction? Which truths?—Human mortality? the illusion of permanence? life's egomaniacal tenacity? No need to lie of these truisms: they're as obvious as dirt.

Consider these pebbles in my sandals, the flies buzzing my sweaty forehead, the fast-evaporating rivulet of urine I've just bequeathed to the backside of the dune against which I'm leaning. Or the incredible, palpable silence of this litorral of the sandsea which laps Cairo from the western, Libyan, desert. A bugspeck hops across my knee. It understands. No Jean-

Paul Sartres needed in the insect world, thank you.  Move your rear as best you can, moment by moment, till the moments aren't.

Art is a creative, unmediated fiction which somehow conveys insight into the depths of being (J. Berger 1986).  A melody, a parable, even a flower arrangement: such lies are prosthetic devices which almost mystically enhance our ability to cull the mass of largely useless knowledge and which thereby reveal heretofore unrecognized patterns.  Art, according to John Berger, is

> an organized response to what Nature allows us to glimpse occasionally.  Art sets out to transform the potential recognition into an unceasing one.  It proclaims man in the hope of receiving a surer reply. . . . The transcendental face of art is always a form of prayer.  (1986)

Because by definition art cannot be mere imitation, the Pyramids—which are, after all, *recreations* of natural wonders—are unsatisfying as art, vaguely irritating.  Nature, being original, is wonderful (which is of course why we wonder about it).   Faux mountains, conversely, are merely disingenuous sandcastles run amok.  Classicism clinging desperately to form out of weakness, dry and hard, authoritarian and cold (Campbell 1972).

"A tribute to the gods!" you protest.  "Divinely inspired, built in ecstatic bliss."

Hoohah.  King What's-His-Name, Hoser, Zozer—whatever—that's who they (attempt to) memorialize.  Kitsch, 2600 B.C.

The L-shaped sand-edge shadow into which I'm wedged shrinks as the morning sun climbs towards an apex.  The quietude is as real a presence as the Pyramid.  Only faint camel groans, distant voices—German, I think—and the buzzing of the circling flies ripple the air.  Far off, to the south, visitors stroll around the manicured, terraced stonepile in assemblages of twos and threes and more.  Almost no one is alone.

A tiny brown spider circumambulates the immense girth of my thigh.  Is it friendly?  Silly question.  The desert, mirroring the sky above, knows plenty of Truth but nothing of niceness.  Hence the fear and loathing of my fellow tourists who instinctively huddle together against the indifference of—not the ersatz peak—the Nothing, the endless, seamless expanse.

As ever, though, fear notwithstanding, curiosity gets the better of them.  Wondering.  If they have a "purpose" that is surely it.  Even the Sahara, the perfect void, needs them.

So do I.  A middle-aged European couple at the base of the Pyramid clamber unsteadily atop a camel.  The woman's echoing laughter heartens us voyeurs, the dunes and the spider and me.  The woman's companion is hanging on determinedly as they disappear 'round the corner of the great form.

The rising heat envelopes me like a narcotic. Warm snakes of sand undulate amidst my toes. The sun drives away a solitary late-morning cloud and my image of the Pyramid suddenly is sharply focused. Like putting on glasses in the middle of an IMAX movie, the finer resolution is momentarily painful. As I stare at it, dazzled and squinting, it seems to project an almost holographic luminescence. Has the Pyramid grown? Surely I can't feel its gravity? Disoriented, I wrench my gaze from this mystery.

I look about for a quite different but equal mystery, a ridiculous three-headed, eight-legged touchstone—the real connection with Zozer and all those who were and will be—bumping across the sands. It, they, must be somewhere on the other side of the Stepped Pyramid of Sikkara. Rising, I follow.


## 2. Iraq—July 1990

**Baghdad**

Approaching Baghdad by air. A stewardess hands me this directive: "Please note that according to the revolutionary command council resolution No. 229 you should call within five days of your arrival to Iraq to the Preventative Health Centre for AIDS laboratory blood tests. Otherwise you will be submitted to a fine of five hundred Iraqi dinars or six months imprisonment in case of not paying the fine." Whew. Kansas this ain't.

Looking about the cabin, I note that the eleven members of my study group are the only non-Arab passengers. We are the objects of frank stares but few smiles. This is quite a departure from the warm humanness to which I've grown accustomed in Cairo. Anti-American hostility or merely cultural difference?

Below, southern Iraq is a limitless vista of rippling ocher dunes and dusty, diffuse horizons. As we near the Tigris-Euphrates valleys, however, the landscape quickly metamorphoses into an agricultural checkerboard: irrigated green fields, small stands of trees, canals, modern highways.

"Looks like Little Rock!" someone cracks. Well, no, but certainly more verdant than, say, my backyard in South Texas at this time of year.

Unlike Egypt, where each landing is an occasion for genuine if raucous cheers, we touch down to absolute silence. The bumpy landing—thermals, I think—does little for my state of mind. What to expect in the home of "the most dangerous man in the world"?

Early afternoon. Crossing the tarmack, I note the temperature: 97°F. Obviously the sun's daily ritual climb has only begun. The new Saddam Hussein (what else?) International Airport is impressively luxurious but so empty it echoes. We are met by our Foreign Ministry hosts, who are as stiffly polite as Oxbridge dons.   The next ten days promise, at the least, to be interesting.

In the first twenty-four hours of my Iraqi visit, I'd encountered Saddam Hussein's name and image at least five hundred times.   It's true that I'm estimating, as I finally stopped counting at "Saddam's Monument to the Qadissya Martyrs" (the quarter-million or so killed in the Iranian war).   I conceded defeat there after observing at that single memorial over 250 photos of Saddam, some of them twelve feet high; a family tree "proving" his kinship to the Prophet; a sketch portraying Hammurabi (yes, that one, the Lawgiver) handing Saddam instructions to continue "our work"; and, finally, after hearing our female tourguide reverence (sorry, but nothing short of this awful nonverb fits) "Saddam Hussein," "our President Saddam Hussein," "our President, His Excellency Saddam Hussein" and (I quote) "the founder of our new civilization, our President, His Excellency Saddam Hussein" more than one hundred times in forty-five minutes.

Although my guide did giggle while explaining the Hammurabi connection, such hyperbole is not uncommon.   The education director of the Student's Union informed me a few days later that "if you cut out our hearts, you'll find Saddam's picture etched into them," and an important member of the National Assembly, in reply to my question about the recent elevation of Saddam to President-for-Life, replied that "our love of His Excellency Saddam Hussein is bigger to us than the machinery of government.   He *is* our life."

The number of billboard-sized photos and portraits of Saddam displayed along Iraqi streets and roads has to be in the thousands.   They must be seen to be believed.   In Baghdad alone, every block is adorned with several.   Immense banners as well: a typical example in Mosul proclaims, "Everybody Loves Our Leader."

My charming Nepali chambermaid finds Iraqis as difficult and as judgmental as Americans.   One of the striking differences I've noticed between Iraq and Egypt, where I've spent the past three weeks, is the Iraqi candor and individualism.   This shouldn't have surprised me, for it was here in Mesopotamia four thousand years ago that the "mythic dissociation" between people and the Divine began.   In India and much of the rest of the East, gods, people, animals, plants and even inanimate matter are all aspects of the indissoluble One.   That notion went extinct in Babylon several millennia ago.   Little wonder that a Hindu maid should find Baghdad as alien as she would, say, Des Moines. From her point of view, it is.

In Egypt, much is made of an ancient Pharonic civilization which turns out to have remarkably little to do with contemporary Egypt, while in Iraq—where days can go by without an intellectual mentioning Babylon, Sumer, Ur or Nineveh—the legacy of Mesopotamia is alive and well.   A staffer at the American embassy offered the theory that the Iraqi character owes to "the Tartar blood."   It is more likely a product of geography—indiscriminate "niceness" hardly seems appropriate in a landlocked desert—and history, especially the early emphasis on material well-being in Sumer, the self-awareness which began in the Mesopotamian city-states and the constant threats from, and frequent invasions by, hostile powers.

Uniquely among Arabs, Iraqis are today direct, prompt, straightforward and quite willing to say no or even "I don't like you." They lie, and smile, only when called for. ("What would be the point of lying, or smiling, otherwise?") Serious, hardworking, unromantic and literalistic, the Iraqis are the Minnesotans of the Middle East. There are worse fates. Irony, as any middle-aged academic can testify, is overrated.

Sunrise over Baghdad from the ninth-story window of my room in the Al Rashid Hotel. Another $45 breakfast. Or is it $3.50? The exchange rate is too screwed up to believe. Officially, the Iraqi dinar is worth about 3.1 dollars, down from 3.8 a few months ago. The black market turns that rate on its head: one dollar buys four or five dinars! The government imposes severe penalties for breaking the currency law and, as I was informed last night at an embassy party, "in Iraq you never know who you're dealing with." (The American embassy is one of a handful which strictly observes the letter of this law, to the considerable disadvantage of the staff.)

The results are predictable. A taxi from the airport to downtown Baghdad is, nominally, $50. One night in a five-star hotel, $250. The first meal of my study group of ten in the Al Rashid—a pretty ordinary luncheon buffet—came to a neat $600. A single banana split is six dinars or $18.

Yesterday's afternoon stroll through the *soq* provided dramatic evidence of the dinar's now-you-see-it-now-you-don't buying power. Ambling through the market, I was repeatedly pulled into closetlike shops where goods were offered—quietly, with much nervous looking over shoulders—for dollars. The opening price for a colorful, room-size Babylonian kilim worth at least one thousand dinars was $100. An exquisite, handcrafted copper jug almost large enough to hold me was $40. As I had no interest in acquiring first-hand experience with the Iraqi penal system, I declined these offers, but it seems that even the items in my backpack were a sort of literal "hard currency." With no pang of conscience, I exchanged my (imitation) Walkman radio for a garnet ring, a miniflashlight for two silver crucifixes, my pocket calculator and a *Time* magazine digital watch for a small rug and two two-ounce bottles of Dewar's scotch whiskey for a 21-year-old, first-day-of-issue Gandhi centenary postcard. My delight was exceeded only by that of my fellow-traders. . .

Eventually, of course, this exercise in self-deception must end. The Iraqis labor under a tremendous debt burden, incurred during the Iranian war, somewhere between fifty billion and eighty billion dollars. Unless the price of oil explodes and remains above $35 per barrel, large amounts of hard currency will have to be gotten the old-fashioned Third-World way, i.e., extracted from Western tourists.  As it is, few American or European visitors will care to pay $15 for a glass of orange juice in Baghdad when the same fresh juice in Cairo is thirty-five cents.

Several members of our group make a practice of loudly belittling Saddam Hussein's vainglory within earshot of our local hosts and five Iraqi embassy drivers.

"You can call him Saddam, or you can call him Saladin (but don't call him Sweetness)!" Nudge, nudge. "Saddam and Hammurabi.  Saddam and Nebuchadnessar.  Saddam and the Prophet!" they bellow.

"Is he real or is he Memorex?  Are they all just great pals, or actually incarnations of One and the Same?  Oooo-weee-oooo!" Gales of raucous laughter.  The rest of us edge away.

Saddam Hussein is an egomaniac (imagine LBJ's ego raised by an order of magnitude), a populist tyrant, possibly "the most dangerous man alive." Still, our group has taken the shilling.  We have come as guests of the Iraqi Foreign Ministry, all expenses paid, eyes wide open.  Is it proper to embarrass these functionaries?  Anyhow, public ridicule of Saddam is punishable by hanging. . .

What do the Iraqis think of Saddam?  Are they afraid of him?  Of course.  His has long been one of the most repressive regimes in the region.  He's gassed his own population of Iraqi Kurds, terrorized the political opposition and, until the last few years, repressed Iraq's Persian Shiia Muslims.  Perhaps one-quarter of a million died in the pointless eight-year war with Iran.  Black-market currency, even laughing at Saddam in public are theoretically capital offences.  Ordinary Iraqis are frightened at the thought of merely being seen talking with Westerners.

So, this means Saddam is unpopular, right?  Yes and no.  Many people on the street favor the social and economic changes.  Except for the burden imposed by the foreign debt, the oil-based economy is strong.  Jobs are so plentiful that expatriates like Egyptians and Indians do much of the manual labor.  Health care and education, even at the universities, is free.

People in Iraq, and other working-class Arabs, identify with Saddam because he began as nothing, threw out the aristocrats, and thumbs his nose at Westerners, Americans especially, whom they believe—rightly enough, let's be fair—to have been biased against Arabs and Muslims for as long as they can remember.

In addition, Iraq is now a state of mind as well as a formal state of being.  Although very heterogeneous and very young, Iraq is fast becoming a nation in the minds of its citizens.  Arabs first, perhaps, but then Iraqis.  This, Saddam's greatest accomplishment, owes to a unifying reverence for the war "martyrs" (borrowed from the Shiias), his imam-like style (and dress, for many street portraits) and, of course, the long Iranian war itself.

Iraq, like Egypt, resists simple-minded analysis. Egypt's people are so irresistibly vital, so extraordinarily human—which other city of fifteen million rivals Cairo's humane warmth and generosity of spirit?—that one finds oneself overlooking another, less pleasant Egyptian reality: its economy. Egypt is mostly desert, has inadequate farmland, and lacks oil; its already-poor population of 55 million may very well be worse off in 2010 when there will be 100 million Egyptians.

Iraqis, who are rather more like the rest of us in human terms, have water, considerable underutilized farmland, a small (18 million) and hard-working population, and Brobdingnagian oil reserves. The Iraqis don't bother with wells producing fewer than 3,000 barrels per day. Earlier this year, the average daily production per well in Texas was under ten barrels. Potentially, this is the Singapore, Germany even, of the Middle East.

Today, between Baghdad and Mosul, two armies streamed by each other, one figurative, one literal. One "army" consisted of thousands of Turkish tank-trucks carrying Iraqi crude to the north. Simultaneously, hundreds of Iraqi Army vehicles of all varieties were heading south, doubtless part of the general mobilization at the Kuwaiti border. A serious dispute over oil has arisen in the last few days between Iraq and Kuwait. Iraq claims that the Kuwaitis have been both exceeding their OPEC quotas and stealing Iraqi petroleum, and that the combined cost to Iraq has been many billions of dollars. (In addition, there is little love lost between Iraq and Kuwait. Iraqis believe that Kuwait should never have been "carved out of Iraq," that Kuwait should have forgiven the fifteen billion dollars loaned to Iraq during the war, and that Kuwaitis tend to be holier-than-thou Muslims at home who behave outrageously in Baghdad and Cairo.)

Saddam Hussein has informed the Kuwaiti government that this situation is "intolerable" and the Kuwaitis—whose entire population is barely twice the size of Iraq's army—are understandably nervous. Still, we and most Iraqis are convinced that Saddam's bellicosity is mere saber-rattling, not the pretext to invasion.

First-hand contact with a repressive cult of personality and expediency like Saddam's is frankly, if somewhat backhandedly, reassuring to an aging academic sour on postmodern America's ability to resurrect archaic ideas like "citizen virtue" and "the common good." If in the Western democracies individualism has run amok—sixty-year-olds wearing braces, The Donald, 2 Live Crew, we all have our own pet awful examples—hope remains, for worthy incarnations have been known to blossom from the nightsoil of self-inflicted pathologies. Consider Scrooge. Something terrific, in other words, may lie on the other side of the alienation and anomie which characterize our current society-wide "dark night of the soul."

Minimally, the individual does still count for quite a lot in the West. Most Americans except, sadly, the poorest and darkest of us can react to the appearance of a police car in the rearview mirror with irritation rather than terror. Moreover, the consequences of our superficiality, our neuroses and our self-centeredness are anything but hidden. We *do* humiliate ourselves with our vulgarity and decadence, embarrass ourselves with ignorance, compulsively consume ourselves, and often—and worst of all, I think—appear determined to trivialize the Land of the Free and Home of the Brave. Still, the very exhibitionistic visibility of these shortcomings; the fact that their effects are largely internalized (in America indirect suicide is still vastly more common than is homicide); our willingness to accept responsibility for our own cupidity (we blame ourselves, not UFO's, for our children's illiteracy); and the extent to which we still respect each other in our daily lives (on the basis of a curiously ad hoc, intuitive faith rather than a defined ethical code), all while, still wishing to be adolescents, we struggle with collective middle-age craziness: this is profoundly hopeful stuff. Kansas may no longer be the Kansas you remember, Toto, but it has stumbled, almost in spite of itself, a mighty step toward those marks of genuine civilization which include the grace to laugh at itself, and to listen.

By contrast, the Oz that is Iraq, notwithstanding the omnipresent smiling portraits, has almost everything going for it—oil, water, small population, work ethic—except the humility of self-effacing humor and the consequent tolerance of difference. These midwestern Middle Easterners could have been the flywheel of a revitalized, reunited Arabic nation. Could yet be. Not, however, by xenophobia and bullying. Those won't cut it any longer.

An Islamic hadith written over seven hundred years ago quotes the Prophet as explaining that he kissed his grandson because, "He who does not show tenderness will not be shown tenderness." That wasn't idealistic hyperbole, it was a prophecy, a forecast eerily realized in a secular, postmodern age. Take a look around, Saddam.

## "Dear Diary"

Dear Diary: Awoke at six to a trio of alarms—wake-up call, room-service buzzer and my travel clock—but somehow we weren't roaring southward till eight. Not a promising sign. Little did I know.

We reached Najaf around ten. Already the temperature was approaching the midday Baghdad readings to which we were growing accustomed, say, 43 degrees Celcius ($\sim 105°F$). The attraction at Najaf is the mosque and sanctuary of Imam Ali Ibn Al-Talib, one of several principal Shiia Muslim pilgrimage sites in the area. The golden dome and minaret shimmered like amber holographs projected by solar lasers, but, alas, we nonbelievers were not permitted even within the courtyard, much less in the mosque where various jewels and other exotica are said to be displayed. Still, the pilgrims were exquisite jewels of another sort, especially the extraordinarily curious urchins; the reclusive, nunlike veiled women; and, the old dervishy men who absently swatted me aside to push into the sanctuary. Even without penetrating the mysteries of Imam Ali's recesses, Dear Diary, I gave Najaf a solid "8."

We pushed on, reaching Karbala near noon. Hotter now, here, than anything we've experienced in Cairo or Baghdad, we find it an effort in concentration to cross the blazing street to the mosque of Imam Hussein bin Ali, second grandson of the Prophet. (The mosque of Mohammed's third grandson, Abbas, is just down the street.) Actually, only Ali's torso is said to rest here in Karbala: his head is in Cairo (or elsewhere. . . much controversy obtains on this subject, better to avoid it).

Double alas, we infidels are again turned aside. Like a campus conclave of Progressive Traditionalists, only true believers need apply. Curious.

Seventy kilometers south of Karbala a stop in mid-afternoon finds us at the Al Ulkhaider Palace. This eighth-century "castle" dates from the peak of Islamic civilization. It is dominated by a great rectangular wall which lends it a fortresslike appearance. One is free to wander through the dozens of rooms within, all of them absolutely empty. The reconstruction of Al Ulkhaider, which begain in 1961, continues.

When I add that the palace lies in the middle of a featureless desert landscape surveyed by the unforgiving Iraqi summer sun, D.D., you will not be surprised when I confess that my principal memory of it was the atomic heat of, at the least, 52°C (122°F, or some such).

It is true that we did doubtless pass other features of interest, but I confess to a certain journeyer's lapse. Out of sorts from thirst—we had last savored a cold drink at breakfast eight hours ago—and traumatized by fear—our government drivers exhibited equally great skill and great stupidity—we, for example, rocketed by, or over, an emerald blotch that must have been Razazah Lake as we searched for the Baghdad highway at 165 KPH (you make the conversion, Dear Diary, I'm too craven). My companion in fear, a political scientist from north Texas, complained as we reentered Baghdad that I'd just taken the Savior's name in vain for the thirty-second time. I apologize. You will be pleased, though, D.D., to learn that I successfully resisted the profound urge to hurl myself from my deathmobile onto Mother Earth—the Al Rashid's concrete drive, actually—thereupon to shower her with grateful kisses.

Yani. (Well.) The A.C. in my room is cranked up (or should I say down?) to the max. There's no one here but me. The audible silence is delicious, sensual. Ilhamdulillah! (Thank God!) There's my $90 room-service lunch at the door now.  In an hour, revisionist braincells co-opted, I'll remember today with a smile.  Yani, maybe a crooked one.

Ma'asalamma, Dear Diary.  Goodbye.


## Leaving Baghdad

Midnight.  A final night in the Fertile Crescent, probably evermore. Alone with my club soda but, for once, resenting solitude.  "Beware what you seek: you may get it."  Fair enough, impossible to argue with such karmic justice.  Why then these thick waves of anticlimax, gelatinous with indifference?  Homeward bound, yet regretful?  Such ingratitude.

Journeys, like lives, appear, enjoy the view for a bit, then, paradoxically, move on.  Grief, some grief, accompanies the close of even the happiest chapter.  This is so, although I cannot say why.  Bitterer far is the close of a story incomplete or a trail unexplored. Is any deathbed anthem so mean as the wallflower's "if only"?

What have I learned? written? been?  Iraq has come and gone and I'm as unchanged as Dorian Gray.  Is this despair?  I think not.  I have persevered, after a fashion.  Made a friend (no small trick, that, for a fiftyish misanthrope).  Grown my awful beard, and trimmed it, too.  Scribbled my scribblings, almost faithfully.  Listened, sometimes.  Perhaps, once or twice, escaped self-awareness, transported elsewhere in moments of beauty and fatigue.  Small stuff, to be sure, but of such stuff are lives raised.

I stroll the Al Rashid's gardens.  It is almost cool out here, barely 90°F, I think.  Manicured flowering shrubs a bit too domesticated, but hints of disorder—an overgrown sign, trees grown too large to keep cutely pruned, rambling, out-of-reach patches of lawn—the ever-lurking chaos of genuine Life.  Resting at a bench by a series of small ornamental reflecting pools linked by four miniature falls, I peer into these nervous mirrors.  They have nothing to say, nothing anyway that I choose to understand.  Even the chorus of the caged waterfalls sighs: no Narcissus, this narcissist.

The sound of John Denver's "Country Roads" wafts across the lawn from the two-man band entertaining the patrons of the hotel's outdoor barbequed-fish (carp Iraqi style) restaurant.  Distracted, my thoughts return to this afternoon's conference, our final official function in Iraq. . . .

We are enduring a two-hour harangue by a deputy director of the General Federation of the Iraqi Women on the evils of Zionism and the cultural biases of the Western media.  This is the hardest line I've encountered among Iraqi bureaucrats.  Is it necessary, I wonder, for women to be ideologically purer, more doctrinaire than men, or is this merely a Baath Party hack?

The Women's Federation facility is one of the humbler we've visited, and surely the hottest. Drenched with sweat, twenty of us occupy a small room "cooled" to 90-plus by one undersized air conditioner. A colleague to my right, none too well to begin with and the oldest member of the study group, is ashen, his eyes wandering like ball bearings.

"The Arab nation," (not "nations"), the deputy drones on, "was the cradle of all civilization." The Chinese, Indians, Japanese and Mayans are going to be upset by this revelation, I muse.

She—the speaker—is an Arab Sophia Loren: same eyes (twin marsh-brown, crystalline almonds), mason-jar mouth, and chipmunk cheeks. Unlike Sophia, but like my wife, her full lips are twin saxonish sausages. The smile is predatory, even cruel, but what the hell.

Our Iraqi protocol man is bewitched too. Staring mindlessly at her, he's wearing the first smile—a foolish grin, actually—I have yet seen on his battered face.

The deputy director continues. "Iraqi women weren't sad when their men were killed in the [Iranian] war. We never encouraged the men who wished to avoid the battlefields. Rather, we pushed them out the door."

At this, the Iraqi man's face falls. He rises without a word and leaves the room. Is she too cold-blooded even for an old infantry officer?

I ask what she thinks of the American feminist tongue-in-cheek (I think) idea of "men as pets." Laughing, she stares at me without the reserve one comes to expect in this part of the world. All right, two can play at this game: I remove my glasses and stare back, dazzling her with the baby blues. Sort of.

She is asked about the 25% cap on female enrollment in the engineering colleges in Baghdad, which we've recently heard explained at the Technical University and the University of Baghdad. Does this disturb her? What quota? she demands. Nonsense! she insists. All university selections are made by computer. Anyhow, Muslim women don't select those fields or specialties which do not allow them to live at home in the city.

Finally, she adds, "However, we'll look into this, just to satisfy our curiosity."

I don't doubt it. Publicly, strictly the party line, but privately, who knows? Heads may roll. I'll remember this tough, persistent, lovely manipulator. . .

I'm transported back to the hotel's garden by a breeze ruffling the branch near my ear. Tomorrow now. Too late for thoughts of today. I mean, yesterday. How much of the Baghdad I remember did I contrive? I wonder, looking toward the dark peak of Al Rashid. The great rosetta—*rashid*—of concrete speaks of nothing except, perhaps, a night's hermitage. That seems enough, now. Leaving Baghdad, I return to my room.

### 3. India—July 1987

## Coromandel

Seated in a chaise lounge belonging to the Silver Sands Resort, I savor my view of the Bay of Bengal in South India.  Behind me lies the hotel's outdoor restaurant-cum-disco, in which five or six teenagers—all boys—are dancing to throbbing pop music.  Their gyrations, which first seemed those of wild abandon, on second glance appear mostly to be self-conscious posturing. Other young men stroll back and forth along the beach, dressed like Californians were in 1970.  Small but athletic, they could be the members of a vacationing Italian soccer team:  just as handsome, graceful, and vain.

Europeans and Russians sit in the shade of the thatched-roof cabanas, drinking canned beer.  They are either overweight or have the studied sleekness one associates with aerobics classes and indoor, one-eighth-mile jogging tracks.  Males and females alike wear bathing suits which verge on the imaginary.

Just fifty yards to the east, a fishing boat puts out to sea.  The craft could be a year old or a thousand:  six small logs lashed together, a homemade sail and two long, crude but effective oars.  Its occupants struggle through a pounding surf, then sail smoothly toward Malaysia.

A vendor walks up the beach, hawking purses.  He is thin, clad only in ancient trousers and nondescript sandals, of indeterminate age:  perhaps thirty, possibly fifty.  A resort guard chases him away from us beautiful people.

Three young women, dressed head to toe in sensible saris, wander down to wade in the shallows.  Unable to evade the clutching tongues of water, they must lift their saris, thereby exposing trim ankles.  Pleased with their daring, they giggle and snatch glances landward to determine if they are drawing the attention they so richly deserve.  Soon, two boys approach, ostensibly to assist them from the water, actually to flirt.  The girls remain proper but are clearly grateful for some attention.  After a bit they return to their table.

Apart from these three, I haven't experienced so exclusively male a scene since Boy Scout camp.  The only Indians in the heavy surf are several hardy adolescent males.  The five rope swings alongside the cabanas hold nine (!) boys in full frolic.  The dance floor, too, is occupied strictly by the preening, prancing males.  Like something out of American Bandstand circa 1959, except here the girls are the wallflowers and the boys dance together.

Several members of our party join the dancers:  three American men, one American woman and one Indian woman.  The local crowd receives them generously, but the Indian boys dance "with" (around, actually) our men rather than the women.  Once or twice the American woman momentarily captures an Indian male but, although flattered and certainly excited, they quickly escape to the security of their mates.

Meanwhile, the three young women sit at their tables and watch. Are they really prisoners of their culture, or is there some key ingredient in this sociological equation which I am missing? I cannot help but watch these watchers and wonder: what are they thinking? What are their whispers when they lean their heads together?

I'll never know. The music blares on, now disco, now Jamaican reggae. The boys—alternately Michael Jackson and John Travolta—spin and orbit, each through his own personal cosmos. The girls, luminescent with beauty and intelligence, look on.


## Toward Ajanta

Through the bus window, I see a young woman squatting in the roadway median. She is unwell. I, too, suffer from cramps and diarrhea. The experience is buffered for me by lomotil, antibiotics, mineral water, soda crackers and—thank God—Pepto Bismol. She has none of these, nor even privacy. In this she is no exception. Millions, mostly children, still defecate themselves to death in India because of unclean water. Millions, each sweating and aching as I am now. Unlike me, however, most of them must feign a public privacy. Like bag ladies in Manhattan, only worse.

As we make a slow turn I see the young woman's face in profile. Tears on her cheeks glisten in the early sunlight. Glancing at our passing bus, she notices and returns my stare. I have managed to rub indignity into discomfort. Ears burning with shame, it is I, not she, who avert my head.

Soon we stop for tea in the town of Sillod, about halfway between Aurangabad and the caves of Ajanta. School children gather around our table to practice their English, whisper excitedly to one another, and simply gaze at these bleached, corpulent strangers. They are genuine, open and absolutely ingenuous. They captivate me and buoy my sagging spirits, like some sort of divine grace. Which, of course, they are.

I teach them to throw my frisbee. At first the girls hang back, but soon several of them are dominating the game. Rather like a nestful of greedy little robins, the children are instinctively covetous in a natural, endearing way. They each clutch, admire, even caress the frisbee before reluctantly sending it airborne once again.

Grateful, I leave the frisbee with the children. It's a selfish thing to do, really, for I hope that a few memories of me linger like a residue in the sturdy plastic of the frisbee.

We proceed on through the timeless Sahayadari hills. Flat-topped plateau remnants stand like sentinels above the rolling upland surface we ply.

The rains have surely been better here than we have seen elsewhere in India, for the earth is a mosaic of many shades of green. There are few evidences of people other than occasional huts and scattered cattle. Unintimidated, this landscape seems poised to return to a previous incarnation.

The caves at Ajanta, by contrast, are profoundly human. Yet they are much more. The twenty-six caves—filled with eerily haunting 2000-year-old Buddhist paintings and sculpture—indent an escarpment of volcanic basalt which stands high above a deep, stream-carved valley.

I recline on the stoop of a monk's cell, temporarily escaping an unforgiving sun. An immense stone Buddha looks down at my disrespectful sprawl with, I fancy, typical tolerance. The hypnotic aria of a waterfall rises from the valley far below. A dragonfly—dragged to these heights by a sudden air current?—stops to gather its bearings and to share the shade. Half asleep, admiring the craftsmanship of the bug's wings, I listen to the rhythm of my heartbeat and to the resonance of the old monks in their ancient caves.

"Maybe we are the illusions and they, or their memories, are the realities," I suggest to my cell-mate. "Or perhaps we're all phantoms, even the valley itself. What do you think?" Weary of passing pedants (after all, insects hereabouts have had millennia to evolve defenses against just this kind of fatuous posturing), the dragonfly flies off.

No matter.    Everything around me—the caves, the paintings and sculpture, the valley, the dragonfly, even the scaring heat—have become clues, guideposts toward some great and continuously unfolding if incomprehensible pattern. I feel my usual relentless self-awareness dissolve into lumpish but delicious langour. Becalmed in the midst of a cyclone of disorientation, thought becomes—what?—being.

Is this, I wonder, enlightenment? Have I somehow transcended the mundane physical world into communion with higher truths? For a moment it seems just possible. . . Then an awesome rumbling of bowels jerks me awake. Oh! I am only dizzy with heat and diarrhea, after all.

With some effort I raise my head to find my fellow travelers, almost all of whom are afflicted with colds, bad stomachs or both. Staggering, leaning, sprawling, with drawn faces: we look like the unfortunate survivors of a two-day fraternity party. Ah well, one more forgettable but human memory for Ajanta's collection.

A devout Mormon professor and our equally moralistic Sikh guide are seated just in front of me during the return journey to Aurangabad. The young Sikh, engaged to be married in a few months, is anxious for a bit of advice and the middle-aged professor seems more than willing to play pundit. Ever ready to fill a breach, I eavesdrop.

"What should a fellow do to impress a new wife with his manliness?" the young man asks.

"Be gentle," my Mormon colleague replies.

"Well," the Sikh continues, "what if I am nervous and unsure of myself on our wedding night. What then?"

"Then," the other tells him, "you must tell your wife exactly that: that you are anxious, even a little frightened. She will repay your honesty and courage with loving gratitude."

The Indian says, "Ah yes, very wise. Now, what should I do if my wife and my mother disagree?"

"Publicly side with your mother, but in private tell your wife that she is correct and that your mother is really quite unreasonable," the western Westerner advises.

"I see, yes. And one final question: what if my wife and my mother join together in a dispute against me, what then?"

I lean forward, interested in the sage's unravelling of this Gordian plight.

"Humm. Well, first, I would thank God for the blessing of a wife and a mother who got along. Then. . . ah. . ." he hesitates.

"And then," calls another eavesdropper, two rows back, "you'd get drunk!"

The two teetotalers exchange looks, laugh, and nod. Grateful for so gracious a conclusion to a day which had started so inauspiciously, I sink into my seat and sleep.


### Peripatetically, Madras

Rays from the newly-risen South Asian sun slant through scudding clouds onto a solitary jogger. Me. "Slogger" would be more like it. My movements reflect all the fluid elan of rigor mortis. My thoughts are so much calcified chatter. For the first time this summer, I am really, truly OLD.

At home, of course, I might remind myself that "you are only as old as you feel." (This is as close as we get to generic mantra.) Indians also claim that age is a state of mind, but—because in the East age is as revered as youth is in the West—they often wish to be older than their years. I think back to a woman in a New York nightclub whom I heard insist to comedian Alan King that sixty is "middle-aged" rather than "old."

"Lady," he replied, "you must run into more 120-year-olds than I do."

What would a New Delhi comic tell a sixty-year-old claiming to be old, except perhaps to "come back when you've grown up. . ."?

Like the Indian notion that all states of consciousness are perfect, even "unpleasant" ones, these seem very pretty principles which nobody actually implements. Or maybe I just feel ancient this morning only because I do not love this state of (semi)consciousness? No doubt both the "middle-aged" New

York lady and her equivalent here in Madras would suggest that my problem is that I am a *kayar*, a coward. They'd be right.

"Nuts: the only universal is that we're all nuts!" I mutter half-audibly, like some muddled escapee lost in shadows. The maze I am caught in is not a mere moor, however. I'm in downtown Madras. Progress through already-crowded streets is a constant struggle of twisting, slowing, even stopping to avoid trucks, cows and still-prone human figures. People are just awakening—taking the morning toilet; leaning to light a fire; simultaneously coughing, talking, and smoking a cheap cigarette; or, mostly, simply sitting on the edge of a "cot" (a blanket spread on the sidewalk), staring vacantly into space. As I pass, the stares shift to me, a satisfactory, if momentary, distraction. As ever (or so it seems to me) Indians seem remarkably tolerant of eccentric behavior. During the course of a run of an hour and a half, I pass thousands of stares, waves and smiles, but few frowns and not a single curse. (Try to match that in Cleveland, Lagos or Paris.)

I ponder this contradiction as I search for the beach. India is a place in which most conform to established values and norms. It is a traditional country. One of the more interesting of these traditions, however, is a certain acceptance of oddball behavior. Consider *sannyasis*: all over India one encounters these spiritual dropouts, elderly men who have left possessions, career and family to wander as saffron-robed beggars, seeking to escape the limits of self before death itself finally comes. In more moralistic cultures (east Asia, say, or central Europe, or even the American middle west) these guys would be considered irresponsible, even parasitic bums. In Hindustan, though, one's highest calling is not a Confucian or Calvinistic sense of duty and responsibility but rather personal enlightenment, a reconciliation with that from which one sprang and to which one will return. As a consequence, Indians can accommodate themselves to all manner of odd public behaviors: urine-drinking prime ministers, naked street-corner swamis, people who eat human flesh, and even joggers. Doubtless this open-mindedness is limited, perhaps even superficial, but it is nevertheless impressive to an intruder from more judgmental shores.

In India, Madras enjoys a reputation for the best of both worlds: competence and efficiency in a languid, tropical setting, a sort of Los Angeles of the Coromandel coast. First impressions reinforce that expectation: a modern, spacious airport; lots of familiar fast-food joints; superhighways; billboard English everywhere (surely more than in, say, Brownsville, Texas); and modern apartments, office buildings and shopping centers—all of it amidst countless palms and flowering tropicals. Stirred, leavened and baked by the alchemy of sun and seabreeze into a pastiche which could never be mistaken for anything other than "Madras." It is beautiful, it is fascinating, and, one fancies, if it is home, there could never be another.

And yet. The chimerical Madras of guidebook and of fond (wishful?) memory—the would-be tropical paradise—suffers badly from our century's peculiar derangement, the conflict we see as that of mankind versus nature but which, here in Hindustan, seems clearly to be us against ourselves and even, ultimately, us against God. Madras is just another of the growing number of tropical cities in which a battle rages between a literally irreplaceable landscape on the one hand and the voracious needs of surging human populations on the other. The results—already evident in the vestiges of Mexico City, Lima, and Cairo, for instance—are sadly predictable. Much of downtown Madras has already become as congested, as dirty, and as indescribably rank as the worst parts of Calcutta. Of the future. . . No, enough of this gloomy reverie. Shaking my head, I reawaken to my surroundings.

Almost out of the business district, I'm confronted with a malodorous drainage ditch occupied equally by debris, mud, and hovels. On the opposite side, however, I encounter a welcome island of greenery, a park filled, to my surprise, with dozens of atheletes-in-training: runners by ones and twos, entire soccer teams, a squad of weight lifters, a pair of boxers. Unlike me, they all seem to be attacking their exercise regimens with Zen-like concentration. Humbled, I scurry across the park toward a sliver of blue on the horizon which can only be the Bay of Bengal. I am anxious to experience the new day at the timeless, warp-and-woof juncture of Indian Ocean with the ocean that is India.

Ocher sands begin half a mile before the beach proper. Like Fort Lauderdale at Spring Break, the cakelike sand is topped with a nearly continuous layer of blanket-swaddled sleepers. Interspersed among them are fishermen tending fires alongside their beached dhows. Ahead, along the water's edge, I can see a line of seated figures facing seaward. I can't yet make them out well, but it seems clear that they are contemplating the orange solar disk, the new day, balanced, like some futuristic atomic beachball, on the sea's rim. As far as I can see up and down the beach, every few yards there is one of these silent, unmoving, iconlike meditators. It is thrilling. "My God," I tell myself, "they're like living Buddhas!" I edge closer to experience firsthand such devotion, such luminescence, such transcendence. Such beauty.

A few tens of meters and I'm at the beach. One ninety-degree turn and, without breaking stride, I am loping along parallel to the pounding surf just to my right and the line of still-squatting, communing figures to my left. They won't take their eyes from their precious sunrise even long enough to register my passage. In fact, although I could be wrong, I have the distinct impression that they are doing their best to ignore me.

"What concentration!" I gasp in awe. "I hate to interrupt such a reverie, but I must learn more of them. Maybe they are all yogis, or swamis, or, I don't know, rishis (do rishis go to the beach for summer holidays?) who'll share profound truths, and teach me of the higher spheres." This may be the very realization I came to India seeking. This is one time I cannot, will not, be a wimp.

I come to a halt by a particularly sagacious, ethereal-looking mystic of indeterminate age. I amble closer, so that this boddisatva (I fancy) squats on his haunches at my feet as though preparing to shine my sneakers. I'm embarrassed by the role reversal, and by the silence. A minute, two minutes pass, and he says nothing.

Finally, I clear my throat. "Ahem." Still nothing.

I plunge on. "Sir, I mean Sri, I couldn't help noticing that you are meditating."

He moves his head just enough to cast a crystalline gaze toward me. "Pardon?" he vibrates.

"Well," I say, "your contemplation. You sit, unmoving, you stare seaward; time passes and you don't even seem to notice. You and all these," I gesture expansively up and down the beach, "these esoteric, these noble colleagues of yours."

"Noble," he slowly repeats, to himself it seems. Turning back to face the rising sun, he continues, "Ah yes: that. It is good to have such a wise visitor among us, for most I think would only have seen our ignobility."

I am confused. "Ignobility?" I ask. "What ignobility?"

Once more he angles his head, this time just sufficiently to see my face. "Why, the defecating, of course."

"What do you mean?" I reply, shaking my head.

He chuckles. "Oh, you're American, aren't you? Well, in your terms, then, it is the 'going to the bathroom' I refer to." Noting my vacant stare, he continues: "Obviously, as you see, although in fact there is no bathroom, we are all here for our morning's toilet. We are defecating."

I can only gape. I back away a pace or two in horror. Then I point an accusing finger. "Why, you're not enlightened. You're not transcendent. You're not even meditating." I am sputtering. "You're just a bunch of defecators!"

Now he couldn't refrain from laughing out loud. But it is a pleasant, avuncular sort of laugh. "No, my friend, you were right the first time. Here, each morning, amidst our ridiculous ignominy, we rediscover sublime nobility. For not only is this the only place we can defecate each morning, it is the best place, for we are literally faced with reminders of what is illusory and what is real. The sea, the wind, the rising sun, the grains of sand beneath my feet, and my fecality and I are all temporary and limited, but we are also parts of a pattern, a continuity which is most heartening." He looks me squarely in the eye. "Don't you think so?"

"I, ah, I must be going now," I reply hastily and, with some difficulty, start my legs moving me away, up the beach.

After a bit, I slow to look back at my tutor. He has resumed his position. He looks just the same, as though I had never been there at all, except for one thing. I can see a small smile playing about his lips. A compassionate smile.

Extracting sand from my shoes, I too begin to smile. This is like something out of "The Three Bears," I think. At first I was convinced that these were special, higher, almost celestial, beings, and I loved them. Then I was equally certain that these were nightmarish creatures, hatefully base and low. Finally, however, like Goldilocks at last tasting the proper porridge, I recognize this particular soup du jour: *Homo sapiens*. Maybe not precisely "just right" but okay. Definitely okay.

Tired, thirsty and overdue at breakfast, I grimace toward the already-blazing sun, and beyond. "All very illuminating, and properly humbling, too," I concede. "But couldn't the dance of Shiva occasionally be a bit less sardonic?"

No reply, of course, to such an ungrateful question.

Crossing the sand toward the city, I pass a fisherman preparing his nets for the day's work. We exchange nods. A favorite melody dances at the edge of memory. Is it Mozart? The Grateful Dead, perhaps. Spirits and knees high, I find that I am running.

## Mysore: Another World

South India's Deccan Plateau is far from the Ganghetic Lowlands of north India, separated by vast expanses of human and physical geography. The contrast is frankly welcome. The great cities of the north, fascinating though they are, are unforgiving in their constant assault on mind and body. Like ant hills somehow trapped in a sauna, the frenzy that is Delhi and Calcutta is as mindless, as wearying and as unrelenting as the heat.

Mysore comes along as abruptly cool, dry and calm as the eye of a storm. The low green hills of the ancient plateau roll on all sides like sleeping emerald snakes. The stolid endurance of these avuncular granites, almost unchanged through a billion years, offers evidence that continuity persists even in the carnival-run-amok that is India.

A warm, tranquilizing sun beats down through the thin atmosphere while a dry, oddly cool breeze rustles the leaves of countless flame trees. The setting could easily be a November afternoon in the Texas Hill Country, except that here the cries of the birds are those of mynas and parakeets.

At sunset, plateau and sky bathed in a riot of pinkish pastels, I jog the Chamudi Hills just outside of Mysore. The few pedestrians are bemused but tolerant as I run their foot- and goat-paths. The crystalline air and the austere but breathtaking highland are heady stuff. Enchanted by the Serengeti-like setting, I prance and canter like (I fancy) a Kenyan marathoner.

People are heading home for dinner now, leading their cattle and riding bikes or bullock carts, or walking in twos or threes. The lights of Mysore sparkle silently below like a stage setting. It is very quiet as I turn to head up to the Lalit Mahal Palace Hotel, now an island of light in this rolling sea of delicious dark.

Earlier I had found Mysore itself to be an island of almost Mediterranean pace and charm. Like the larger Bangalore located just to the north, Mysore is an affluent "garden city." Countless trees and flowers provide welcome first visual and olfactory impressions for the newly arrived.

Bangalore was at one time even lovelier than Mysore, but unchecked population expansion is eroding this beauty. Bangalore's residents brag that it is the fastest growing city on earth: 2.9 million in 1981, almost 5 million now, perhaps 10 million by the year 2000.

Thirty years ago Mexico City was also a place of haunting loveliness. So too, in varying degrees, were Lima, Rio de Janeiro, Guadalajara, Buenos Aires and Cairo. Today it is impossible to visit these cities without despairing that there seems no going back. . .

By comparison, the smaller Mysore (of perhaps 400,000 inhabitants) still shines like a lustrous pearl. Its boulevards are wide and the drivers almost tame (emphasis on the "almost"). There are many green cricket and soccer fields, parks, several public gardens, and a fine zoo. The architecture is turn-of-the-century British colonial amalgamated with turn-of-the-century Mysore maharaja. The wonderful fruit-and-flower market is busy, but the ubiquitous frenetic crowding of most of the rest of urban India is absent.

Mysore has easily the largest and most visible middle class I've encountered in India. These people live in tidy private bungalows and cottages, many of which have their own neatly manicured yards and gardens (itself a rarity in India, aside from the very well to-do). The predominantly youthful people on the streets have a surprisingly Western look, particularly the males: "University of Budweiser" t-shirts, jeans, sneakers, even backpacks. Only the middle-aged women, old men and Hindu sadhus always wear the traditional dhotis, saris and kurtas.

The city conjures up thoughts of Bologna and Florence. These people seem to have that rare ability to capture the best of modern and traditional. Their pace is unhurried but functional. Like Italians, I think, Mysore's inhabitants tread admirably that thin line between passivity and compulsion.

Outside the Cottage Industries Emporium, hawkers sell old coins, anklets with sensuous little bells, coral necklaces, and lots of junk. A boy of perhaps ten sells me a "very special" Buddha amulet. An almost spherical little lady offers a silver belt for three hundred rupees. I walk away, feigning disinterest. We enjoy the dance of on-again-off-again negotiation over many blocks and one hour. We settle on seventy rupees. Other vendors—maybe a dozen—gather around, offering more treasures. They tease, cajole, laugh, argue; they rarely take offense and never grovel. I am enchanted.

In the fruit-and-flower market, a Muslim perfumier straight out of the fourteenth century demonstrates his wares. I stop merely to admire his flasks of jasmine, frangipani, lotus and a hundred others. Soon, having somehow ordered ten different perfumes, I watch transfixed as the alchemist fills, and his young apprentice labels, each vial. Unasked, they serve me a "single char," a small cup of sweet, milky, and very hot tea. Fragrances of perfumes and flowers float almost visibly about my head like bouquets of ghosts. I sit dazed on a stool in a forgotten corner of the world, surprised that mindless anonymity could feel so good. Reluctantly, I pull myself away so the poor guy can go on making his living.

As I wander through the bazaar, I stop to admire the old coins an ancient, bearded holy man has spread before him. Included is a very weathered fifty-paisa Gandhi piece, one which seems to me just the coin the Mahatma himself might have carried. The sadhu asks for one rupee, an embarrassingly fair price. Having only a 100-rupee note, I ask him to hold it for me while I go to search for change in the market (always a challenge in India).

"No," the old sage says. "I may be gone then. If you like it, please take it."

His Indian generosity equalled by my American avarice, I do. He smiles.

The sadhu's gift remains a treasured legacy of Mysore and of Gandhi but, most of all, of one particular shining soul. . .


## 4. England—August 1987


**Beloved Muddlers**


London. Lord, how easy it is to revert to being Anglo Saxon. English people, like English weather, may be chilly and austere but they are mine.

I sit feeding the pigeons in Paddington Station. These are without question the scruffiest pigeons I've ever seen. The ragged little birds bob and peck around my feet like so many sad chickens. One drags a mangled left foot. They are all dirty, stupid little creatures, as unprincipled as seagulls. Why, then, am I so fond of them?

The English sit waiting for trains to beach resorts where they'll sit under cold, cloudy, even drizzling skies, somehow successfully conjuring imaginary sunshine. We are all munching ginger biscuits and scones and white-bread sandwiches, drinking sodas from litre bottles or tea from thermoses.   (At 9:30, it has been an hour and a half since breakfast. Naturally, we consider ourselves famished. . .)  We read *The Star* or a Danielle Steele novel, or we speak quietly (immediate family, of course, not strangers), or we simply gaze rather contentedly at the activity about us.  It feels good to be stupid and free from normal responsibilities for a bit.

There must be homelier people than we, but none come readily to mind.  Most of us are just a pasty-faced, doughy variety of "plain," but not a few are caricatures straight out of Dickens:  warts, bad teeth, knobby hands, club feet, wandering eyes, even hunchbacks.  Frankly, the best looking of us wouldn't turn a head on the steets of Milano, Paris or Rio.

We ARE a clean and tidy lot, though.  Oh, there are I suppose plenty of unkempt orange-haired "punks" among us, but these are really rather boring.  It is the anonymous seniors who are interesting.  For those over thirty-five, I think, tidinesss is a badge of honor.  Sit in the lobby of a Salvation Army hotel such as the Red Shield, where most of the permanent residents are old men living on small pensions.  In the United States, most of these fellows would be bums:  dirty, smelly, often hopeless drunks.  Some of these drink to excess, too, but—until very near the end—theirs is a more private, more dignified despair.  They arise early, they clean themselves, they brush their painfully threadbare suits, they read the morning papers.  In this regard they seem to me to be more like American women than men.  They pretend that the answer to Hamlet's question is "to be" even when it is not.

Still, this is not the compulsive neatness and orderliness of the Germans.  These English know full well how easy and how pleasant it would be to slip off into oblivion.  These are, at least at some level, calculated rituals.  However alone, they rise, wash and dress each morning; they dine sitting at table with cups and plates and saucers (rather than from cans, while standing) as a gesture of defiance.  In the face of a seemingly unfair, even cruel cosmos, their silly grace suggests a curious, unspoken faith that, as Einstein put it, "God doesn't play dice with the Universe."  No wonder they and the Indians understood one another.

The English skies are leaden, drizzly and cool; it is perhaps 65°F.  Two days in London and I've already caught a cold.  I almost enjoy these aching ears, though, and this raspy throat.  I KNOW I enjoy wearing a wool sweater, sleeping under a thick comforter and drinking endless cups of REAL tea.

London is deliciously quiet after Calcutta, Bombay and Delhi.  Even Picadilly Circus at midday is silent by comparison, mainly because horn-honking is not here considered a form of artistic self-expression. . .

Even better is the wonderful anonymity.  The English don't stare at, follow, or even register a foreigner on the streets.  Another time I might take this to be a sign of an indifferent, uncaring people.  Now, I could kiss them for their very distance.

Britons are not, of course, completely unlike Indians. Both are survivors, muddlers; both are indirect compared with Americans (although if the Indians are translucent, the English must be opaque); and—contrary to conventional wisdom—they share a bent for the material, the visceral, rather than the cerebral. (A period in excess of one hour without eating at least something is, in both countries, considered to be virtually the onset of a fast.) How, I muse, can one dislike such human human beings?

Cleve Hill. Mid-August, but already there's a bit of autumn in the air here in the Cotswolds. The first yellowed leaves are carried about by a stiff north wind. I wish in vain for an evening fire in this Cleve Hill youth hostel ("If we start the fires now, they'll be going till May!").

The rolling green hills seem timeless at first glance, but of course they have been profoundly changed by human occupancy for four millennia or so. The original forest cover has long since been cleared for sheep grazing, farms, villages, homes, and countless gardens.

Rather like a Japanese bonzai garden, in the end the manicured Midlands countryside leaves one grieving for its lost wildness. At least in India—which has been just as thoroughly stripped of naturalness—the natural world is clearly only held at bay, ever ready for just enough assistance from the four horsemen to allow it to reclaim its rightful place.

The tourist's England is now so quaint, so, well, cute, that it has the instant charm of a slumbering infant. India is more like a hungry baby with dirty diapers AND the colic: you hate it, you love it, but you never like it.

I walk through a cold drizzle to the village of Winchcombe. Too weak to play tourist, I catch the bus to Cheltenham. It is really too cold for my single jumper, so I amble into the nearest Oxfam thrift shop to search out another sweater. Instead, I purchase a polyester suit for 95 pence. Nobody wears polyester suits, but 95 pence!?

My map indicates that I can visit both Burton-on-the-Water and Stow-on-the-Wold with one bus ride. Who could resist such an opportunity? In Stow, a professionally quaint village, I sit sipping tea, watching other visitors stroll slowly through a steady downpour. Middle-aged couples whose children are newly gone, I decide. These people are far more affluent than their Indian counterparts (and, again, far homelier) but eminently likeable for some of the same reasons. They are hopeful souls. They do their best. They don't penalize those about them for their sufferings. Frail, but rarely broken. Is this courage or merely ignorant stolidity? I am convinced that, for both Indians and English, it is the former.

The sun has freshly broken through and I am drawn to the streets. As I step out of the tea shop in a stupor of smug benevolence, I am promptly buffeted to the sidewalk by pedestrians coming from both directions. I had forgotten this peculiarly English quirk, this Anglo-Saxon equivalent of the blaring horns of India: the absence of sidewalk body-language. In London,

Birmingham, Edinborough, even Stow-on-the-Wold, pedestrians plow along, heads down, bumping and popping off one another like so many kernels of popcorn. "Sorry," they mutter autonomically, "so sorry," and plow on. Sprawled just now across the sidewalk, my parcels and I are the traffic obstruction, for example, but still we hear: "Sorry, terribly sorry." "Doubtless," I growl to myself, "if this box were in the middle of the desert they'd (a) trip over it and (b) apologize to the damned thing!"

   I am bruised, tired, and a little sick. Still, it is pleasant to lean for awhile against the nearest wall, soaking up both the wan sunlight and the bustle of my passing cousins. I experience a rush of gratitude for the summer's exposure to such a multitude of dazzling, intrepid spirits. It begins to drizzle once again. A very large woman waddles by, leaning close to speak to her amused husband. A little boy stands crying, staring at the ice-cream cone he's just dropped onto the pavement. An old gent leans on me momentarily, then, gathering his resources, pushes open the door of the bookmaker's shop with his walking stick. Stuffing some cotton into my ears, I push off the wall, joining the flow of this parade of life. It's time to go home.

# List of References

Abbey, E. 1968. *Desert Solitaire*. Tuscon, AZ: Univ. of Arizona Press.

Adler, M. 1990. *Intellect: Mind Over Matter*. New York: Macmillan.

Bachelard, G. [1934] 1968. *The Philosophy of the New Scientific Mind*. Tr. G. C. Waterston. New York: Orion.

Bakko, E. 1989. Dominion means servitude. *Saint Olaf* July/August: 3-5.

Barley, N. [c 1983] 1992. *The Innocent Anthropologist: notes from a Mud Hut*. New York: Holt.

Barzun, J. 1989. *The Culture We Deserve*. Middletown, CT: Wesleyan Univ. Press.

———. 1990. "Toward a Fateful Serenity." In *Living Philosophies*. See Fadiman 1990.

Bateson, G. 1972. *Steps to an Ecology of Mind*. New York: Ballantine.

———. 1979. *Mind and Nature*. Des Plaines, IL: Bantam.

Berger, J. 1985. *Restoring the Earth*. New York: Knopf.

———. 1986. The white bird. *Harper's* 272:33.

Berger, P. L. 1981. *The Other Side of God*. New York: Anchor Books.

Berman, M. 1981. *The Reenchantment of the World*. Ithaca, NY: Cornell Univ. Press.

Berry, W. 1970. "Secular Pilgrimage." *A Continuous Harmony*. New York: Harcourt Brace Jovanovich.

———. 1977. *The Unsettling of America: Culture and Agriculture*. New York: Avon.

Bhaskar, R. 1989. *Reclaiming Reality: A Critical Introduction to Contemporary Philosophy*. London: Verso.

Blakney, R. B. 1941. *Meister Eckhart: A Modern Translation*. New York: Harper & Brothers.

Bohm, D. 1971. *Quantum Theory and Beyond*. Cambridge: Cambridge Univ. Press.

———. 1980. *Wholeness and the Implicate Order*. London: Routledge & Kegan Paul.

———. 1988. "Postmodern Science and a Postmodern World." In *The Reenchantment of Science*. See Griffin 1988a.

———. 1989. Neutrons feel a subtle quantum effect. *New Scientist* 123:28.

Born, M. 1936. *The Restless Universe*. New York: Harper.

Boulding, K. 1980. Science: our common heritage. *Science* 207(4433): 831-836.

———. 1990. Personal communication with author.

Bouquet, A. C. 1962. *Comparative Religion*. Harmondsworth, Middlesex, Eng.: Penguin.

Branwyn, G. 1991. The salon virtual. *Utne Reader* 44 (Mar/Apr): 87.

Brody, H. 1982. *Maps and Dreams*. New York: Pantheon Books.

Brown, L. 1990. *The State of the World, 1990.* New York: W. W. Norton.

Buber, M. 1958. *I and Thou.* 2nd ed., trans. R. G. Smith. New York: Scribner.

Buechner, F. 1973. *Wishful Thinking.* New York: Harper & Row.

Burton, I. 1991. Banquet speech 5 March. Houston Area Research Center Conference on Global Warming and the Regions. The Woodlands, TX: Houston Advanced Research Center.

Byatt, A. S. 1990. *Possession.* New York: Random House.

Campbell, J. 1972. *Myths to Live By.* New York: Bantam.

Capra, F. [1975] 1983. *The Tao of Physics.* New York: Bantam.

———. 1982. *The Turning Point.* New York: Simon & Schuster.

Cendrars, B. 1970. *Moravagine.* Garden City, NY: Doubleday Projections Books.

Chaffetz, D. 1981. *A Journey in Afghanistan.* Chicago: Univ. of Chicago Press.

Chan, W.-T. 1963. *A Source Book in Chinese Philosophy.* Princeton: Princeton Univ. Press.

Chatwin, B. 1977. *In Patagonia.* New York: Summit Books.

Chesterton, G. K. 1926. *Orthodoxy.* London: John Lane The Bodley Head.

Cobb, J., Jr. 1988. Ecology, science, and religion: Toward a postmodern worldview. In *The Reenchantment of Science. See* Griffin 1988a.

Codrescu, A. 1990. *The Disappearance of the Outside.* Reading, MA: Addison-Wesley.

Commins, S., and R. Linscott. 1954. *Man and Spirit: The Speculative Philosophy*; and *Man and Universe: The Philosophers of Science.* New York: Pocket Books.

Conner, S. 1989. *Postmodernist Culture.* Cambridge, MA: Basil Blackwell Ltd.

Daly, H. E. 1973. *Toward a Steady State Economy.* San Francisco: W. H. Freeman.

Davenport, G. 1981. *The Geography of the Imagination.* San Francisco: North Point.

The Decline of New York. 1990. *Time* 17 Sept., 38.

Durant, W. 1961. *The Story of Philosophy.* New York: Pocket Books.

Eckermann, J. 1930. *Conversations of Goethe.* London: J. M. Dent.

Eco, H. 1989. *Foucault's Pendulum.* New York: Harcourt Brace Jovanovich.

Eiseley, Loren. 1946. *The Immense Journey.* New York: Random House.

Fadiman, C., ed. 1990. *Living Philosophies.* New York: Doubleday.

Ferguson, M. 1980. *The Aquarian Conspiracy.* Los Angeles: J. P. Tarcher, Inc.

Ferre, F. 1988. "Religious World Modeling and Postmodern Science." In *The Reenchantment of Science. See* Griffin 1988a.

Ferris, T. 1985. *Creation of the Universe.* (Video.) Washington, DC: PBS Video.

———. 1988. *Coming of Age in the Milky Way.* New York: Morrow.

Fletcher, C. 1988. A bend in the road. *Wilderness* (Winter): 12-16.

Foucault, M. 1983. *This is Not a Pipe.* Berkeley: Univ. of California Press.

Fukuyama, F. 1989. The end of history. *The National Interest.* Summer.

Garvey, J. 1991. Of several minds. *Commonweal* 25 Jan: 41.

Geyer, G. A. 1990. Welcome to the dangerous post-cold war world. *Corpus Christi Caller-Times*, August 26.

Gleick, J. 1987. *Chaos: Making a New Science.* New York: Viking-Penguin.

Goldberg, N. 1986. *Writing Down the Bones.* Boston: Shambala Publications.

Gould, P. 1990. Personal communication with author. Aug. 14.

*Granta.* 1984. Travel writing, vol. 10.

———. 1987. The story-teller, vol. 21; With your tongue down my throat, vol. 22.

Griffin, D. R. 1988a. Ed. and "Introduction: The Reenchantment of Science." *The Reenchantment of Science: Postmodern Proposals.* Albany: State Univ. of New York Press.

———. 1988b. "Of Minds and Molecules: Postmodern Medicine in a Psychosomatic Universe." In *The Reenchantment of Science. See* Griffin 1988a.

————. 1990. Personal communication with author.

Haggett, P. 1990. *The Geographer's Art*. Oxford: Basil Blackwell.

Hanh, T. N. 1987. *The Miracle of Mindfulness*. Boston: Beacon.

Hardison, O. B. 1989. *Disappearing Through the Skylight*. New York: Viking.

Harman, W. 1988. "The Postmodern Heresy: Consciousness as Causal." In *The Reenchantment of Science. See* Griffin 1988a.

Hassan, I. 1975. *Paracriticisms: Seven Speculations of the Times*. Urbana: Univ. of Illinois Press.

Havelock, E. 1963. *Preface to Plato*. Cambridge: Harvard Univ. Press.

Heisenberg, W. 1970. *Natural Law and the Structure of Matter*. London: The Rebel Press.

Heller, A. 1990. *Can Modernity Survive?* Berkeley: Univ. of California Press.

Hesse, H. [1922] 1951. *Siddhartha*. Trans. Hilda Rosner. New York: New Directions.

Holmes, R. 1984. In Stevenson's footsteps. *Granta* 10.

Holmes, S. 1988. The community trap. *New Republic* 28 November, 24-26.

Hooson, D. 1991. Clarence Glacken: In Memoriam. *Annals of the American Geographers* 81(1):157.

Horn, M. 1989. The legacy of cubism. *U.S. News and World Report* 23 October, 68.

Horwitz, T. 1991. *Baghdad Without A Map*. New York: Penguin.

Howard, M. 1985. The bewildered American raj. *Harper's* 270: 55-60.

Jackson, R. L. 1981. *The Art of Dostoevsky*. Princeton: Princeton Univ. Press.

James, W. [1902] 1958. *The Varieties of Religious Experience*. New York: Mentor, New American Library.

Kapleau, P. 1966. *The Three Pillars of Zen*. New York: Harper & Row.

Khan, H. I. 1978. *The Complete Sayings of Hazrat Inayat Khan*. New Lebanon, NY: Sufi Order Publications.

Khan, P. V. I. 1981. *The Call of the Dervish*. Lebunon Springs, NY: Sufi Order Pub.

King, I. 1989a. Quantum reality, chaos, and the social sciences. President's Annual Meeting, National Social Science Assoc. New Orleans, LA, Nov. 2-4.

————. 1989b. Personal communication with author.

————. Undated. "Political Economy and the 'Laws of Beauty': Aesthetics, Economics and Materialism in the Thought of Karl Marx." Conway, AR: Department of Political Science, Hendrix College.

Klinkenborg, V. 1991. *The Last Fine Time*. New York: Knopf.

Koestler, A. 1952. *The Arrow in the Blue*. London: Hutchinson. (Reprint 1969).

————. 1978. *Janus*. New York: Random House.

Koppel, T. 1986. Media courtesans. *Harper's* 272: 18-19.

Korzybski, A. [1933] 1958. *Science and Sanity*. International Non-Aristotelian Library, III, 4.

Krishnamurti, J. 1970. *Think on These Things*. New York: Harper & Row, Perennial Library.

————. 1989. With a silent mind. *Newsletter of the Krishnamurti Foundation of America*. Ojai, CA: Krishnamurti Foundation of America.

————. 1990. *Newsletter of the Krishnamurti Foundation of America* Fall/Winter. Ojai, CA: Krishnamurti Foundation of America.

Kundera, M. 1984. *The Unbearable Lightness of Being*. New York: Harper Colophon Books.

Laing, R. D. 1976. *The Facts of Life*. New York: Ballantine.

Lasch, C. 1979. *The Culture of Narcissism*. New York: W. W. Norton Co.

LeShan, L. 1974. *How to Meditate*. New York: Bantam.

Levene, M. 1984. *Arthur Koestler*. New York: Frederick Ungar.

Lowenthal, D. 1986. *The Past is a Foreign Country*. Cambridge, Eng.: Cambridge Univ. Press

McCarthy, C. 1992. *All the Pretty Horses*. New York: Knopf.

Maddocks, M. 1990. I am not an intellectual. *World Monitor*, August: 80.

Mann, T. 1948. *Doctor Faustus*. New York: Alfred Knopf.

———. 1955. *Confessions of Felix Krull*. New York: Alfred Knopf.

Meadows, D. 1988. "Quality of Life." *Earth '88: Changing Geographic Perspectives*. Washington, DC: National Geographic Society.

Mearsheimer, J. 1990. After the Cold War: Will we miss it? *Current* 327 (November).

Milbrath, L. 1989. *Envisioning a Sustainable Society: Learning Our Way Out*. Albany: State Univ. of New York Press.

Miller, E. L. 1972. *God and Reason*. New York: Macmillan.

Miller, M. C. 1985. America's telescreens. *Harper's* 270: 25-28.

Miller, R. 1989. The earth system: Human dimensions. *The Global Forum*. Washington, DC: National Science Foundation.

Monod, J. 1972. *Chance and Necessity*. New York: Vintage.

Morris, J. 1980. *Destinations*. New York: Oxford.

Muir, J. [1912] 1989. *Yosemite*. Madison, WI: Univ. of Wisconsin Press.

Munro, E. 1987. *On Glory Roads*. New York: Thames & Hudson.

Murdoch, I. 1954. *Under the Net*. New York: Viking.

Myers, M. 1975. *The Assignment*. Don Mills, Ontario: PaperJacks.

Nagel, T. 1986. *The View from Nowhere*. New York: Oxford.

*NEA Today*. 1990. November.

Needleman, J. 1970. *The New Religions*. New York: E. P. Dutton.

Niebuhr, R. 1937. *Beyond Tragedy*. New York: Macmillan.

Norwine, J., and A. Gonzalez. 1988. *The Third World: States of Mind and Being*. London: Unwin-Hyman.

Ornstein, R., and P. Ehrlich, 1989. *New World, New Mind*. New York: Doubleday.

O'Rourke, P. J. 1988. *Holidays in Hell*. New York: Atlantic Monthly Press.

Pascal, B. [1844] 1952. *Pensées*. *Great Books of the Western World*. No.33. Chicago: Encyclopedia Brittanica, Inc.

Paz, O. 1989. Time's voice. *New Republic* Nov. 6: 95-98.

———. 1990. Mankind's destination should be plurality, not uniformity. *Houston Chronicle*, Oct. 21.

Picard, M. [1934]. 1989. *The Flight from God*. Washington, DC: Regnery Gateway.

———. 1952. *The World of Silence*. Chicago: Henry Regnery Co.

Pirsig, R. 1974. *Zen and the Art of Motorcycle Maintenance: Or An Inquiriy Into Values*. New York: William Morrow.

Popper, K. 1975. *The Philosophy of Karl Popper*. LaSalle, IL: Open Court.

Popper, K., and J. Eccles. 1984. *The Self and Its Brain*. London: Routledge.

Pribram, K. 1976. *Consciousness and the Brain*. New York: Plenum.

———. 1977. *Perceiving, Acting and Knowing*. Hillsdale, NJ: Laurence Eribaum Assoc.

———. 1978. Karl Pribram's changing reality. *Human Behavior* 7:28-33.

———. 1979. Holographic memory. *Psychology Today* 12:70-73.

———. 1980. The role of analogy in transcending limits in the brain sciences. *Daedalus* 109:19.

———. 1982. Interview with Karl Pribram. *Omni* 5:128.

Prigogine, I. 1972. Thermodynamics of evolution. *Physics Today* 25 Nov.

Prigogine, I., and I. Stengers. 1984. *Order Out of Chaos*. Boulder, CO: New Science Library.

Radhakrishnan, S., and C. A. Moore. 1957. "The Mahabharata." *A Source Book in Indian Philosophy*. Princeton: Princeton Univ. Press.

Raeburn, P. 1991. U. S. gains in some science. *Corpus Christi Caller-Times*, Feb. 17.

Ralston, H. 1979. "Nature and Human Emotions." *Understanding Human Emotions*. Bowling Green, OH: Bowling Green State Univ. Studies in Applied Philosophy.

Rappole, J. 1989. Personal communication with author.

Rifkin, J., and T. Howard. 1989. *Entropy: Into the Greenhouse World*. New York: Bantam.

Rousseau, J. J. [1781] 1945. *The Confessions of Jean Jacques Rousseau*. New York: Modern Library.

Rowell, G. 1986. *Mountain Light: In Search of the Dynamic Landscape*. San Francisco: Yolla Bolly Press, Sierra Club Books.

Ruckelshaus, W. 1989. Toward a sustainable world. *Scientific American* Sept., 166-174.

Rucker, R. 1983. *The 57th Franz Kafka*. New York: Ace Books.

Sartre, J.-P. 1966. *Being and Nothingness*. Trans. Hazel E. Barnes. New York: Washington Square Press.

Scruton, R. 1980. *The Meaning of Conservatism*. London: Macmillan.

Short, J. R. 1992. Mythos, logos and community. Paper presented at Annual Meeting, Assoc. of American Geographers. San Diego, CA: Dept. of Geography, Syracuse Univ., Syracuse, NY.

Sperry, R. 1981. Changing priorities. *Annual Review of Neuroscience* 4:1-10.

———. 1987. Structure and significance of the consciousness revolution. *Journal of Mind and Behavior* 8,1:37-66.

Steegmuller, F. 1972. *Flaubert in Egypt: A Sensibility on Tour*. Boston: Little, Brown & Co.

Steiner, G. 1989. *Real Presences*. Chicago: Univ. of Chicago Press.

———. 1990. "Struck Dumb." In *Living Philosophies*. See Fadiman 1990.

Stonebarger, B. 1985. *The Soul of Science*. (Video.) Madison, WI: Hawkhill Assoc., Inc.

Storr, A. 1988. *Solitude*. New York: Free Press.

Stuart, D. 1990. The sine qua non for a post-modern coalescence of science and religion. Conference on Science, Technology, and Religious Ideas. Kentucky State Univ., March 6-7.

Symanski, R. 1990. *Outback Rambling*. Tempe, AZ: Univ. of Arizona Press.

Thomas, L. 1990. "What I Think." In *Living Philosophies*. See Fadiman 1990.

Thompson, W. 1987. *Gaia: A Way of Knowing--Political Implications of the New Biology*. New York: Inner Traditions--Lindisfarne.

Tinker, G. 1988. Indian spirituality and the American university. Edward Mattingly Symposium on "Share the Nebraska Tribal Experience." Nebraska Wesleyan University, Lincoln, March 25.

Toulmin, S. 1982. *The Return to Cosmology: Postmodern Science and the Theology of Nature*. Berkeley: Univ. of California Press.

———. 1990. *Cosmopolis: The Hidden Agenda of Modernity*. New York: Free Press.

Tuan, Y.-F. 1970. Our treatment of the environment in ideal and actuality. *American Scientist* 58:244-249.

———. 1972. Structuralism, existentialism, and environmental perception. *Environment and Behavior* Sept., 319-330.

———. 1978. Sign and metaphor. *Annals of the Assoc. American Geographers* 68: 266-276.

———. 1984. Continuity and discontinuity. *Geographical Review* 74: 245-256.

———. 1989a. Surface phenomena and aesthetic experience. *Annals Assoc. of American Geographers* 79(2): 233-241.

———. 1989b. Personal communication to the author, 6 Nov.

————. 1990a. *Yi-Fu Tuan's Monthly Newsletter*. 6, no.7 (Dec. 1). Madison: Dept. of Geography, Univ. of Wisconsin.

————. 1990b. Realism and fantasy in art, history and geography. *Annals of the Assoc. of American Geographers* 80 (3): 441-444.

————. 1990c. Personal letter to author, August 13.

Vidal, G. 1986. *Creation*. New York: Ballantine.

Watts, A. 1970. *Nature, Man and Woman*. New York: Random House-Vintage.

Weil, S. 1952. *The Need for Roots*. New York: G. P. Putnam's.

————. 1965. *Seventy Letters*. Trans. Sir Richard Rees. New York: Oxford.

Wheeler, J. 1973. "From Relativity to Mutability." In J. Mehra, ed., *The Physicist's Conception of Nature*. Dordreicht-Holland: D. Reidel.

White, L. 1967. The historical roots of our ecological crisis. *Science* 155: 1203-1207.

White, T. H. 1958. *The Once and Future King*. New York: Putnam.

Will, G. 1990. Arab nations: tribes with flags. *Houston Chronicle*, Aug. 8.

Wolf, L. 1990. Personal communication with author.

Zaehner, R. C. 1989. *Zen, Drugs and Mysticism*. Lanham, MD: UPA.

Zeitterling, M. 1989. "Mai Zeitterling Stockholm" (videorecording). New York: Learning Corp. of America.

# Index

# About the Author

Jim Norwine, Professor of Geosciences at Texas A&I University, specializes in physical geography, climate and science education; he also teaches Oriental philosophy. He was named the university's Distinguished Alumni Research Professor in 1983. The author of numerous scholarly articles and essays, he has been elected an Explorers Club Fellow and a member of the scientific research society Sigma Xi, and was the recipient of a National Endowment for the Humanities fellowship to Columbia University (Asian literature). Norwine has spent periods in India and Yugoslavia as a Fulbright Scholar and in Egypt and Iraq as a Malone Fellow. He and his wife Lottie live in Kingsville, Texas. *A Postmodern Tao* is his fourth book.